I0161546

AN ECONOMY OF WORDS

A collection of poems by

Bob Myers

NORTHWEST
PASSAGE
Books

Gatineau, Quebec, Canada

An Economy of Words

by Bob Myers

Copyright © 2018 by Bob Myers. All rights reserved.

ISBN: 978-0-9939527-7-7

Published by
Northwest Passage Books
Gatineau, Quebec, Canada

Cover photo by Brendan Myers.

(Third printing, January 2026)

*This collection is dedicated to my wife Linda,
our seven children and fifteen grandchildren.
Inspirations all.*

TABLE OF CONTENTS

Publisher's Foreword

If you are not one of the author's nearest friends or family members, then this foreword is for you.

We would like to know how you found this book. We were planning a very small print run, to be given as gifts to a handful of the author's nearest and dearest. Did you find it at a charity sale, or in a box in someone's basement? Was it holding up the short leg of a table? Or hidden under the cushions of an old chair, where someone accidentally dropped it? We'd like to know. For one thing, we'd like to track down that rotten sod who lost this book or gave it away, and demand from him an explanation. It had better be a good one. For this book is the author's heart.

Bob Myers was born 1945 in county Laois, Ireland: a part of the country where, as he says, "the tourists never go". His childhood consisted in getting lost in fairy rings on the way to school, hiding from the BanShee (that's how he pronounced it) whose comb he had found on the road, and wondering what the kids in the Protestant school looked like. He came to Canada when he was eleven years old, studied English at the University of Guelph, got married, became a school principal, and bought a house in Elora to raise his seven children and they all turned out mostly fine. The rest of the details, you shall have to figure out for yourself by reading the poems.

He says they're about ordinary events. Nevertheless, here's over seventy years of them: some beautiful, some disturbing, and some deeply weird. Together they are his memoirs in verse, his autobiography in art, his voice crying out in the desert, his celebration of the ordinary life. And that is no ordinary thing.

Now, the observant reader will notice that in the first sentence of this book of poetry, a book which happens by non-coincidence to be full of poems, Myers denies being a poet. What a strange lack of grasp upon reality! In fact I wonder what other features of his world have not been approved by the Committee. For in this book you will find fairy stories, ghost stories, stories of childhood's follies and elderhood's nostalgia, love songs, travellers tales, fragments of conversations with the souls of others and the soul of the world, delivered with the irony and dry whimsey of Stuart McLean or Stephen Leacock. But it's not the ghosts which are the problem. It's his style of whimsey, isn't it? You'd have to know the sound of his voice to get the whole effect. Without it, some of this stuff — the first few lines of *Penance,* for example — might sound a little creepy. As for most of the rest of it: well, in this modern age we are supposed to be self-absorbed and cynical! So, I am withholding one last poem from the collection. Our modern age doesn't deserve it. It's quite irrelevant that his last poem is a recipe for barbecued ribs with honey-mustard sauce. I'm keeping it for myself. Unless this book is in the running for a literary prize. Then I might share it with the judges.

You will also notice, because you are probably not blind, that many of these poems are also works of serious Christian devotion. Myers is the sort of Catholic whose Catholicism is sometimes too much for other Catholics. He is too fun-loving and intellectually curious for the puritans: for him, God is "in my flower garden / playing with my child." A sentiment like that is worthy of Kalil Gibran. At the same time he is too conservative and ethically uncompromising for the reformers: this same god will dispense "direful justice" in the *Endtimes*. Since you've already read this far into the preface, you might as well know where all this religious intensity comes from. Of course he was religious from a young age. But in his midlife, his body became host to several incurable viruses with unpronounceable names. These microscopic monsters traded his bodily energy for a constant background of physical pain. His religious faith was his rock in the weary land. It allowed him to see how everything in the world has its place in the choir — including his suffering. These poems are his testament of a faith that allowed him to turn his frustration and anxiety into art. I dare say that his endurance of his physical disabilities (slogging along the

Camino Sketches, for example), his perseverance through a traumatic childhood (see *Contrition*), his integrity in the face of social ostracism (see *Kitchen Photos*), the preservation of his generosity and his sense of wonder throughout, is the kind of quiet heroism for which other men have been beatified.

He wouldn't want that, though. He would likely settle for seeing a copy of this book on a friend's bedside table, dog-eared, coffee stained, scribbled full of notes — evidence that it made someone happy for a while.

All right, then. Enough about the man. Enough of this prologue, too. Time to sum up.

If you've wondered what it would be like to visit a world full of ghosts and fairies and angels, where people spend long afternoons eating big home-cooked meals, drinking good wine, and arguing about the wherefores and the whytos of things, and where a nearby God presides over everything, well then here's your book. And if the style of these poems isn't modern enough for your taste, that's okay. This book wasn't meant for you anyway. Drop it off at a charity shop. Maybe someone will pay two dollars for it, and maybe there's a medical researcher who needs the money.

But first, consider the following. This book is my father's heart. By way of some wandering path through time and space, it has landed in your hands. Maybe there's something in it that was meant for you, after all.

Brendan Myers
Publisher, Northwest Passage Books
March, 2018

AN ECONOMY OF WORDS

PREFACE

I am not a poet. I make that clear in the first entry, which is called Fly Fishing. I am by profession a teacher who loves to read and teach poetry and finds great pleasure in writing poetry to please myself and maybe my family and friends. In this collection you will read about my faith and some principles I embrace, about family, friends and people encountered, about ordinary things and ordinary events that pepper all our lives.

I have borrowed from Scripture and favourite poets without claiming them to be mine and have found in some Psalms an opportunity for comment. Inspired by the Japanese Haiku form, I have come up with a challenging structure which is in my opinion a great exercise for anyone who likes to express themselves in writing. These Encuigries* are made up of five lines of twenty words and twenty-five syllables, with line two and five rhyming, lines three and four rhyming and two questions asked. The syllables must be distributed as three, four, five, six, seven from the first through to the last line respectively. There is no restriction on subject matter so find pen and paper and get started.

---

* From the English word *enquiry*, and the Irish word for the number five, *cuig.*

There was always a library in our home containing literature, history, art, reference, and current fiction and non-fiction, and reading was encouraged. So was expression and debate around the dinner table, on the porch on warm Summer nights, on vacation trips and wherever there was a news item or gossip worthy of disagreement. As a result, four of our children became published writers and performed playwrights, and the pressure was on me. Whenever they found scraps of paper with something I had written, they said I should put them into a collection. I have finally taken that advice for most of my efforts. Some are meant for other eyes only.

But I am not, with respect to expressive writing, a vain person. My writings are not my legacy.

My legacy is my family whom I love dearly.

Full stop!

Bob Myers
February, 2018

FAITH AND PHILOSOPHY

Fly Fishing

At the river's edge
big Sean wouldn't let me go in
until he read the water.
I surveyed the flood line,
and being tall and thin,
thought I could be swept away

like a grey-haired dandelion
if I slipped or fell.
I heard him say
something about nymphs and hatch
and rubbing a little jell
on dry flies, and how to play

the wind to my favour, to cast
on the current letting the line drift
to the pool where the fish were.
In waders two sizes too big,
all I could do was shift
my weight across moss covered

rocks, feel the current tug my legs,
play my balance, catch my breath.
Foothold gained, a compelling
urge to look upstream made me turn.
A dazzling fiery stretch
of morning sun, blazing

like a bellowed furnace, burned
my sight to blindness in a flash.
Less circumspect I might have felt
a momentary compassion for Lot's wife.
Downstream, his understated triumph and a splash.
Sean said there was an etiquette

to fly fishing. You spared the fish his life,
caught and released him just
for the sport then sported the river again.
A romance with water and trout.
And there he stood, caught
in his dreamy refrain,

carefully coaxing the line out
in the clear mountain air,
weaving the silken web over
his head, then letting it gently float
onto the languorous surface where,
almost carelessly, it hovers,

as soft as an intimate whisper
on a lover's heart. Lean as I am
I cannot unknot my body
as he does to master
such liquidity of limb.
I wield a mechanical stick; he

is poetic elemental man.
I battle with balance and time
like a ham-handed fisherman.
Blinded by Heaney and Yeats.
Casting for rhyme.

The Door

Quiet the voices inside this place!
Dampen the candles! Quickly! Haste!
Bring the bar down, the shutters secure,
nor stir the fire to blaze and grow.
This is no night for beggar or king
when thieves and wolves are holed in their den
and the moon rules over a treeless moor
and the cold stars wish for a blanket of snow.
For whispers and rumours from shadows and mist
creep over the threshold and cling like dust.
As the midnight hour encircles our fears
the sound of a beast draws fearfully near,
and its keeper pounds on the door with his fist
and we steel ourselves to die if we must.
But listen! Listen! It must be so!
The voice of a woman in some distress!
And the turmoil tightens within our breasts.

The Man Who Invented Dreams

He was cold born
at dawn,
naked and cold
as a featherless bird.

When he saw
the sun rise,
he rose too
and felt its warmth.

At midday
(how could he know?)
his first words;
sounds inside himself,
so he ate something
and drank something.

Later, he explored,
witnessed,
listened,
smelled,
touched.
No questions,
no answers,
just experiences.

At sunset
he too lay down,
closed his eyes
and felt a caress
beneath his heart.

Then he slept
to dream of her.

II

And this is
the dream he dreamed.
He dreamt
he saw himself

More comely,
more glowing,
most pleasing to look upon,
most desirable of all creatures.

In his dream
they did not speak
(Did they not yet know words?)
but together walked
to a still water
and saw themselves

naked without shame
and beautiful.
They touched
her softness,
his angularity,
the pool reflecting
his formidability,
her grace.

In his dream,
the first and everlasting
dream of man,
he felt something;
a longing for.

And when he awoke,
she was.

III

The man saw his wife
for the first time,
the woman who had
been brought to him

as he slept
and dreamed.
At last he spoke to her
who was like him.

In his joy he
called her
"flesh from Adam's flesh,"
(For was not Adam man?)
because he had
been given words.

He named the living
woman "Eve"
and brought her
around the garden
of delights.
He said,
"This is ours
and its creatures are ours.
Our Lord
the God who
fashioned us
gave this to us
for our pleasure.

All except the fruit
of that tree."

IV

But Eve was
proud and vain.
She wanted more.
She desired knowledge.

She saw,
smelled,
touched,
longed for the fruit.

A serpent said,
"you may eat."
(Isn't the tree yours?)
So she
and Adam ate
the forbidden fruit.

They said,
"but we are naked!
Let us cover ourselves.
Let us hide ourselves,
our shame
from God
in the trees
in silence."

It was evening.
As God was walking
in the garden
He found them
hiding in the shame

of their nakedness
and sin.

V

"I ate the fruit
to gain knowledge
to be godly
like you.

The serpent
said it was good
so I ate," said Eve.
"And Adam ate."

God punished
Adam and Eve
(Hadn't they disobeyed?)
The serpent
He condemned
to crawl in the dust.

God banished
the man and his wife
from the garden
of heavenly delights,
from the paradise
made for them
in His love
for them.

Thereafter Eve laboured
in pain at childbirth.
Adam laboured
at breaking the soil.
And when he slept

he dreamed.
He dreamed restlessly.

Spring Snow: A Wisdom Poem

Just when you think
you've got it all figured out,
when you notice the days getting longer,
sunshine frequenting the blueing March skies
and cleansing rain washing Winter
from roofs and roads;
just when you think
Winter's back is broken
and you can begin to include
the word "Spring" in your corner conversations,
and you notice the tips of
Spring bulbs cautiously poking
out of the semi-frozen ground,
and because you wished for these things to happen
that they came into being
as if you were the one
responsible for these changes,
and you think you are,
comes a rogue North wind
with its cargo of Spring snow
and a brace of cold, cold, days
and the voice of the Creator
carried on grey-black clouds:
"Who is this obscuring my designs
with his empty-headed words?
Tell me, since you are so well informed!
Have you visited the place where the snow is kept,
or seen where the hail is stored up?
What womb brings forth the ice
and gives birth to the frost of heaven?
Do you really want to reverse my judgment,
and put me in the wrong to put yourself
in the right?"

Just when you think
there is no end to your weariness
and your present travail has never been
borne by anyone before,
that escape from the oppressive burden of daily
concerns have been denied you for so long
that only you know the true nature of grief,
when your spirit is
drawn and parched and spent
like your body at the end
of a hot Summer day
and no amount of rest can bring relief,
comes a mild West wind
with its rapture of soothing sleep
on an evening of cool, cool, rain
and the sigh of the Creator
carried on downy wings:
"Who makes grass spring
where everything was dry?
Has the rain a father?
Who begets dewdrops?
Come, you must set your heart right.
You will forget your sufferings,
remember them as waters that have passed away."

Just when you think
that you've solved the mystery of life
and you're feeling full satisfied with your lot,
like the blanket of well-being
that wraps around you
at the end of a perfect meal,
when you savour all the glory that is you,
family, friends, a warm hearth, good health,
the glow that starts from within
and migrates slowly into every living cell
as surely as the constant
furnace of the sun animates
all living things;

just when this surety
of self-reliance is safely
secured in your soul,
comes the tender caress of the breath
you felt when He held you in His hands
and called you by your name:
"Can you claim to grasp the mystery of God?
This state of things is all of God's own making.
He holds in His power the soul of every living thing
and the breath of each man's body.
Turn your mind to praising His works
and meditate on His wonders."

Bread And Wine

You'll find no bones in bread.
I who knead the dough
with measured roll and pull,
massage and work and blend
the malleable knob,
love the living swell,
the buttermilk and flour's
alluring bittersweet
redolence, who form
the blessing cross across
the dough hereby declare
the bonelessness of bread.

Wine, when from the fruit
pressed, expressed and poured
like a living libation,
a living stuff that breathes,
matures, improves with age,
draws from sun and soil,
from lineage and stock
nobility of race.
Elixir of brigands and kings,
intoxicant sublime,
in its agreeableness
does everything but bleed.

*'"*This is my body given*"*
in the Galilean hills,
at the table of the twelve,
apportioned for my people
fastened to a tree like a boneless hide.
*"*This is my blood shed*"*
like a wineskin splattered,
split upon the stone,
cleansing soil and soul.
Manna for the hungry.
Life for those who thirst.

Suffered Under Pontius Pilate

I   Pilate

Long before they came to claim
one of theirs was quite insane
calling Yahweh as his own
Abba, Father, Holy One,
forging a conspiracy,
learned Scribes and Pharisees
conjured wicked plans and doom
circumventing those to whom
courage was a two-edged fault.

Pontius Pilate's cautious wife,
soothing one more fitful night,
whispered to his tumult mind
well considered words and kind,
not so politic as warm,
neither urgent nor alarm
but as honey from the heart;
"E'er this evil night departs
be in mercy unreserved.

Look beyond their devious schemes,
hear and harken to my dream.
Let them have no cause to say
the Roman Governor delayed
issuing a just command
executing any man
who would wear in Caesar's place
the kingly crown of his own race.
His blood is theirs, theirs be his blood."

Words left ringing in his ear,
"devious…..execution." Fear
of a sudden formed a chance
for his favour to advance
in the sight of Roman eyes,
while the ones whom he despised,
spurred into a frenzied mob,
carry out this sordid job
so his office bore no stain.

Thus he hastened to the throng
with his wife to think upon
how he would a law proclaim
in the power of Caesar's name.
Then, to satisfy their lust
(tempered by her counsel first)
forged in dreams and passion's fire,
"He will die at your desire."
And they clamoured for His life.

II   Law and Order

A justice who was one of eighty-three
posted to the Empire's arid edge,
bored by wearisome monotony
and the plodding pace of powerlessness,
when summoned to attend the hours to come
within the smoky light of oil and flame
that brought but little cheer to prison dome,
heard a fellow toiler call his name
and rent him from his dream of Tuscan skies.
"Friend, let us place a wager, something small,
to keep a tally of His tortuous plight.
And if He dies, well, one of us takes all.

I know this cohort and its officers,
an ill-reputed lot, I've heard it said,
who make good sport of boasting, as it were,
that they can play a man 'till nearly dead.
Note the soldier bending by the fire,
a poultice held beside his wounded face.
The man's disfigured, having lost an ear
when swords were drawn, and acting in much haste
to make a swift arrest, failed to see
an errant blade thrust in the crowded yard.
He'll seek revenge, I'll bet, most terribly.
What say you friend? Shall we risk ten denar'?"

The prisoner is fastened to the stone
surrounded by the wounded warrior's men.
A vicious scourging then is laid upon
by brute and brawn who relish in His pain.
And when exhausted by their heavy blows,
they pass around the junk-embedded rod,
at thirty-nine, and not a flicker more,
the cataract of punishment is paused.
"They seem intent on following the law.
A course which falls with favour to your hand.
Here, take these coins, you've won the opening draw,
and I am naught, if not an honest man."

An eerie fog of heavy silence falls
across the jackals and their carnage but
is broken by a startled voice that calls,
"Look at my ear! Look at my ear! The cut
is gone! It's gone! The blood and pain are gone!
He touched me! I remember how he drew
His hand across my face……. the wound is gone!
His followers were talking of a new
and glorious kingdom where He would be king.
But when they saw us coming to arrest
Him, they turned tail and didn't do a thing.
And yet, He heals a man he should detest."

A skin of wine is pressed into his grasp.
"I trust you're not having any doubts?
There's nothing kingly to this common trash.
Before we've done with Him we'll make Him shout
and beg the mercy of a swifter death!"
Emboldened by this more familiar talk
Their appetite for lust and gore is whet.
Across His lacerated back a cloak
is thrown, and for His head a crown of thorns
is fastened to His scalp and firmly fit.
Then where upon His frame no wound is borne,
they honour Him with kick and blow and spit.
Now ridicule and mockery join the fray
as if this pack of dogs can't get enough.
Shouting, cursing, taunting, punching, they
don't understand His failure to rebuff.
"How goes the tally, friend? They move so fast.
To mark the number of each blow's a guess.
I can't keep up. It seems to me that last
one brings my count to sixty-six at least.
I've grown accustomed to this wicked work.
I've drawn these hours more times that I recall.
But this one's different, all reason's lost.
What drives this man? He just…..endures it all!"

"My orders state that He's to be released
after we have done our duty well.
Pilate wants Him chastised for the peace,
but He's still ours and this is still His hell!
Press that crown around His royal eyes,
bind the thorns unto that noble head.
Pull His beard and hair to make Him rise
so we can worship Him before He's dead!
Treat Him with respect now, don't offend
the eternal gods. The gossip is He told
His questioners that He would, in the end
reign in a kingdom of another world."

Officials of the palace guard approach
with documents to carry Him away.
The dungeon crew, now weary of their sport
return His robes, then leave without delay.
"Looks like they'll execute Him after all.
Those wicked wounds! And such a loss of blood!
I bet He won't get far before He falls.
Let's call the wager off. I think they should
dispatch Him by the sword, despite His crime.
I have no stomach left, I'm off to bathe.
Now doubt I'll feel much better in due time.
And yet, and yet, is justice not betrayed?"

III   Claudia

Claudia could find no rest
only anguish and distress,
everlasting hours of grief
and the fear of haunted sleep.
Desperate efforts to retrace
what was written on His face
as she stood by Pilate's side
Listening to their callous lies.
What had made her feel so small?

Maybe it was how He met
Pilate's calculated threat
that a gesture of his hand
sent a firm and swift command
to pacify provincial strife
by forfeiting the prisoner's life.
"You would have no power over me
were it not granted from above.

The greater guilt must be assumed
by him who handed me to you."
She pondered less of whom He spoke

that how her spirit bore the yoke
of this invasion of her soul.
What was the value of the whole
world if she could not come to know
the place He was prepared to go
even at the highest price?

Well she knew his weak resolve,
how he used the law to solve
the difficulties that arose.
The punishment, he had supposed,
would help reverse his failing luck.
But when they called on ancient books
he washed his hands and turned his head.
"I wish he was the man I wed,
that proud and most ambitious knight."

Even as he sent the writ
he called his wife and bade her sit
to hear his private thoughts expressed.
"I listened to His words, and yes,
I find it is, the risk be known,
impossible to just disown
that He might be the Son of God.
Remember how the one called John
deeply puzzled Herod's mind?"

IV   The Road to Golgotha

A practiced team of soldiers roughly bind
the heavy Patibulum to His back
and outstretched arms, then prodding Him in line,
begin the long parade along the path
towards the gate that opens where a hill
called Golgotha looks back upon the town.
The scorn of mankind, jest of wise and ill,
staggers awkwardly then pitches down,
a violent fall against a stony road.

Tax collectors, prostitutes and thieves,
merchants, lawyers, money changers goad
and loudly cheer as He bears their grief.

They toss their mocking heads and sneer again
as crashing to the ground He hits the stones
a second time. His face is mangled when
it grinds into the dirt beneath the load.
Utterly exhausted there He lies
a broken, bloodied outcast, while the crowd
along the route assail Him with their cries.
A soldier's blow tells Him He's not allowed
to catch His breath, but now He is too weak
to answer their commands, and so they force
a bystander to help Him gain His feet
and share the weighty beam along the course.

Outside the town the grade presents a climb
for able-bodied men to undertake.
For Him a mountain looks, and every time
He takes a step His limbs and bones are raked
with piercing jolts of unrelenting pain.
Each foot of ground is gained under a moan
as flesh and sinew tear against the frame
until his shoulder opens to the bone.
A misplaced step propels Him to His knees,
another soldier's urgent kick is paid.
He meets a pair of eyes and hears the plea,
"Can we go home now, Mamma, I'm afraid."

Once more the stranger helps Him to His feet,
a crippled swaying body of a thing
surrounded by a herd of bulls who see
to leave Him lying in the dusty ring.
They glare at Him, they laugh at Him, they gloat,
their spittle clinging to His bloodied face.
"If Yahweh is His friend, then Yahweh ought
to rescue Him and take Him from this place."

Some dance and bow before Him in their praise,
"King of the Jews, son of our fathers' God,
you're not much of a king or son these days!"
And still His weary way He onward plods.

Befitting of this scene where anguish lies,
like a creeping cloak of ashen grey
comes a flood of cloud across the skies,
a tide of doom upon a wicked day.
A crowd excited by a spectacle
fails to recognize a thing apart,
when everywhere the gloom and clamour spells
an evil born in emptiness of heart.
He, and He along, perceives the cry
as tender as a blessing from above,
"My son, my son, turn to me so that I
may carry you upon a mother's love."

He lifts His head and finds her soothing smile
a shelter in the shadow of the storm,
a golden spear of love, a honeyed wine
flowing like a precious healing balm.
A sudden whip, the nightmare is renewed,
His enemies won't let Him be consoled.
No sympathy impairs a hostile mood
that fuels itself on ridicule and scorn.
But mercy, like a gauntlet hurtled down,
brings a sudden standstill to the pace.
A maid steps in His way, and with her towel,
wipes the toil and torture from His face.

The lust to see the gibbet clasp His form
peaks upon the final stretch of road.
Frenzied citizens and men-at-arms
compete for favoured space to watch the show.
But here it was that in Jerusalem
noblewomen gathered in the crowd
with sweetened drinks for men who were condemned,

on seeing His demeanour wept aloud.
Among the mourners, one of rank and race,
of unmistaken confidence and pride,
touched His memory of another place,
a woman standing at her husband's side.

Three men were cruelly crucified today,
the most degrading death a man could die.
Two thieves and one who stumbled on His way,
whose guilt was that He didn't fit the crime.
Compelled by law and duty to attend,
a weary justice, a centurion,
review the task from start to grizzly end,
in passive rote and cold indifference.
The soldiers close their ranks to form a wall.
A mother and some friends decide to stay.
A leaden dome of darkness starts to fall.
The wolves begin encircling their prey.

V Epiphany

The fortress of Antonia
looks out over Golgotha
like a mighty sentinel.
In his efforts to dispel
torment from his troubled mind,
Pilate found himself inclined
to climb the lofty western tower
when at the appointed hour,
Jesus would be crucified.

His was not an easy road.
By the final right of sword
every Prefect understood
Rome was blind to he who could
keep the peace with Roman might.
Power invites one to exploit,
and in his fall from grace he used

bribery, outrage, theft, abuse,
until his conduct reached an ear.

The sudden coolness of a breeze
sent a warning up his sleeve;
a change of weather would ensue.
"Soon they'll crucify me too
but what awaits me I deserve.
And the masters that we serve,
where will they be when we meet
our ignominious defeat?"
Pilate in his solitude.

She leaned against a stony wall
and she let her shoulders fall,
closed her eyes and tried to find
the very moment He passed by,
the very heartbeat when He stirred
a longing she could not ignore,
like a craving in her breast
that promised nothing but unrest
and a hunger for the truth.

VI   Crucifixion

I see your flesh-embedded garments torn,
your bloodied body hurtled to the ground,
the executioner kneeling on your arm,
the gloating aristocracy aroused.
I watch the heavy mallet drive the nail
with sudden piercing pain into your wrist.
A second blow, the other limb impaled,
your hands begin to spasm and to twitch.

"O Lord, how is it we can be so blind
as not to see the offence of our eyes?
I gaze upon your broken form and find
your arms outstretched to free those doomed to die."

I hear the soldiers cursing as they strain
to lift the beam and fix it into place
atop the upright post, and curse again
the politics of temple and of race.
"If you're King of the Jews, then save yourself,"
they laugh and raucously deride,
and when they tire of insolent contempt,
they raise another cross on either side.

"O Lord, how is it we can be so deaf
as not to hear the offence of our ears?
I listen to your enemies confess
their lack of faith, their secret hidden fears."

I pause to contemplate the span of time
you hung upon that most dishonoured tree.
Hour on endless hour you were consigned
to repetitious torture, when to breathe
or speak you had to push yourself upright
until exhausted muscles disobey
and slow asphyxiation wins the fight
crumbling your frail humanity.

"O Lord, how is it we are so unwise,
as not to hold each precious moment dear?
Unfettered by restraint, we sacrifice
the present promise of eternity."

A thief, one of the two abused and swore,
"Are you not the Christ? Then save yourself
and us as well." But you spoke not a word.
Such is the verdict of the world of men.
But friendship and salvation must be earned.
The other wretch, who found himself inclined
to faith in you, won paradise in turn.
You stoop to raise the lowest of mankind.

"O Lord, how is it we can be so poor
as not to know your mercy everywhere?
Surely you could not have loved us more?
Surely you have borne our grief and care."

A tide of darkness falls across the land,
the sun is covered, day becomes like night.
A superstitious soldier's trembling hand
loosens and lets fall a clutch of dice.
"I thirst…I thirst," they hear your feeble plea,
a dirty sponge is dipped into a bowl
of wine and myrrh to ease your agony.
Do they not know your thirst is for men's souls?

"O Lord, how is it we should live apart
risking all for some uncertain prize?
Teach us to understand you with our heart
and know whereby the road to heaven lies."

How much longer can you go on like this?
Overpowered by violence and ruin.
And yet your mercy burns with tenderness,
your passion like a desert flush with bloom:
a mother's child is met with tranquil peace,
a restless heart begins to bless your name,
a man condemned to torment is released,
another held your cross without complaint.

"O Lord, you shed on us abundant grace,
that sweet libation soothing all distress.
In its alarm, this sin-tormented race,
cries for rescue from its wickedness.

The final hour. "Come down from the cross..
you would rebuild the temple in three days!"
This shame, this horror, this inglorious loss
of promise leaves your friends in disarray.
Pity turns to doubt, doubt to despairing

yet even onto death, your love prevails.
"This is your mother…" and by her submission
to your will, hope is restored again.

"O Lord, we don't deserve to be your brother.
We look for miracles to prove your might.
Show us by the fiat of our mother
the virtues of a simple humble life."

The heavens shake, the earth in anger quakes.
"Into your hands my spirit I commend."
The temple veil from top to bottom tears.
"It is accomplished, " and bowing your head
you breathe your last. When the Centurion
saw all these occurrences take place
he praised God saying this man was His Son.
The spectacle has ended. Go in peace.

Listen all you heavens, earth attend,
take your evil ways out of His sight.
Your arrogance will be brought to an end,
The Risen Lord shines forth His saving light!

———————————-

"Let the records indicate
we neither love nor tolerate
those who serve us as they choose."
Caligula was not amused.
Bound by duty and an oath,
Pilate fell upon his sword
long before his worthy wife
found conversion in her life
and the holy name of saint.

Easter Song

We are an Easter people,
Springtime's holy dew
waking the world
from its darkness,
God's people old and new.

We are a people rejoicing
singing our allelu,
filling the air
with our gladness,
God's people old and new.

We are the broken and feeble
tossed like a pair of old shoes
into society's
dustbin,
God's people old and new.

We are the children of innocence
slaughtered inside the womb,
the criminals of
inconvenience,
God's people old and new.

We are the sons of forgiveness
freed of our sinful dues,
unworthy heirs
of His mercy,
God's people old and new.

We are an Easter people,
God's people old and new.
We are beloved
of the Father,
the light of His eyes. We are you.

Finches At Easter

Like golden blessings
falling from heaven
they suddenly arrive,
dozens of yellow finches,
wings flapping, colliding,
overlapping, feathers
fluttering, scuffling
on the seed box,
a tremulous tumble
of yellow delight.

In the midst
of this Spring fling,
a startling slash of purple
transfixes my gaze;
a single reference-point
purple finch
suffering their abuses.

Behind these gossamer curtains
I am close enough
to touch.
I dare not breathe.
Just stand and watch.

Transfixed.

Troubled at his
undeserved torment.

Elated by their
spirited vitality.

The Shower

Me
on showers.
This regular ritual
is a blessing for some.
Called to the power
of cleanliness we come,
heavy-eyed navigators of unfamiliar
dawn, groping for a light switch,
balancing the hot/cold flow
of water, setting shampoo and soap bar
at hand before stepping behind
the curtain, leaving the weary world outside
to enter the sweet embrace
that washes body, soul and mind.
This is not a passive exercise.
One must skillfully unbend limbs,
turning, stretching, reaching,
decreasing in order to harmonize
flesh and water
into a symphony of lovely liquid joy.
In a moment, sleep's heavy burden
rises like laughter.
Yesterday's dust and decay
are swept like an
irresistible tide
once and forever away.
Lord, in your unfathomable mercy, come
cleanse me of my sins.
Let your grace pour upon
me as each day begins.
Shower on
me.

And Life Everlasting

In darkness all the peoples call
for brightness, for your coming light.
They grope in darkness and they fall
seeking the radiance of your sight.

The First Day

And then the seeds of doubt begin to grow
like little whispering worms to lure away
their confidence and courage. "Did He not say
the place where I am going, you cannot go?"
"Have we been left behind to face the Jews?"
"What did He mean, 'Rebuild the temple in
three days?' And how on earth can He begin
at suffering and death to make things new?"

The worms invade the recesses of the mind
and spin a web of fear around each heart
that saw the promise of His life depart
in shame and horror, thus it is they hide
behind closed doors, beneath the city's gloom,
this chosen band, afraid to face their fears,
has nothing left to give but bitter tears
spawned by whispers in their prison room.

A troubled heart becomes a heart of clay
lost in grief and lifeless as a stone.
A failing lamplight flickers on alone
against the dawning of another day.
The once beloved rises from the floor,
he wants someone to say it isn't true.
While others cling to slumber, only two
hear the cautious closing of a door.

The First Song of Magdalene

She can't remember
when she came
to rise above
her pride and shame,
to seek The Way
that everywhere was rumoured.
Maybe she was
drawn to Him,
or maybe it was
just a whim,
a desperate chance
that He might listen to her.

How she struggled
in her soul!
How she longed
to be made whole,
to come to terms
with pain and grief and suffering.
All the healers
had run dry,
all the gods
had made her cry.
Neither wealth nor prayer
could conquer dying.

Yesterday
she heard them say
in a town
not far away
He had healed
a soldier's ailing servant.
Now that Jesus
and His friends

were coming
to Jerusalem,
was she seeking
hope or desperation?

Tortured by
demonic pain,
with Salome's help
she gained
a corner of the courtyard
where He might be.
From behind
the pressing crowd,
as He passes
she has found
the courage to call out,
"I am not worthy."

In a moment
all are gone
and an old
familiar song
rises to her lips
just like a whisper.
From her eyes
a veil of tears
springs to laughter
and the years
of doubt are banished
now and ever after.

The Second Day

The hours before the Sabbath numbered three,
too brief a span to satisfy the rites
of burial, but Pilate said they might
in haste, entomb the body as agreed.
One hundred pounds of myrrh served as balm,

two body lengths of new Sodara shroud
stretched from head to toe, and then around
Othonia linen bound the rigid form.

Under supervisors sent to prove
the tomb was sealed, the ritual complete,
sentries at arms stood on to meet
any covert plans to have Him moved.
Neither Nicodemus nor the guards,
nor Joseph who laid Jesus in the cave,
knew the presence of a heart so brave
as Mary peering from the garden yard.

The lamplight fails. Peter beckons John
alerted by the lifting of the latch.
It was, they guess, a changing of the guard,
the last before the night gives way to dawn.
An anxious Magdalene begins to run
with Mary and Salome close behind.
And when they reach the tomb, it shock they find
blinded soldiers and His body gone.

The Second Song of Magdalene

Such a lovely
afternoon.
In the heat
she nearly swoons
overcome
by torrents of emotion.
Promises
to sacrifice,
change the focus
of her life,
like a fragrant
flower of conversion.

For a woman
to disclaim
rank of family
and name,
tending an
inflammatory preacher,
brought another
kind of trial,
homelessness
and self-denial,
servitude
discipleship would teach her.

Whence this rush
of overtures?
All He gave her
was a cure
as a countersign
to her distresses.
Placed His hand
upon her head,
looked into
her eyes and said,
"Mary,"
and continued the procession.

There's a longing
she had known,
there's a yearning
that has grown
like a heavy
weight of suffocation.
From henceforth
she is restored
by the calling
of her Lord,
she who sowed in tears
now reaps rejoicing.

Comes again
that simple song
when she was a little one,
something about
love that lasts forever;
"Hush, my lamb,
my heart's delight,
let your sorrows
all take flight,
let them fall on me,
my love, my treasure."

The Third Day

A sudden crash! The holy spices spill
across the holy ground, and as she weeps,
an angel comes to her and kindly speaks,
"Why look among the dead for He who lives?
Don't you recall the Son of Man had to
be crucified by sinful men and rise
on the third day?" Mary lowers her eyes
and trembling with fear prepares to go.

On the path she meets another man.
Thinking Him the gardner she implores
  that He direct her where to find her Lord.
She does not recognize nor understand.
She feels His living breath upon her cheek.
She sees the love shine from His living eyes.
She hears Him whisper, "Mary" like a sigh
that promises an everlasting peace.

Joy is fairly bursting from her breast
as the women race to tell the news.
But the disbelief and ridicule
of the others causes them unrest.
Only John and Peter dare to leave

and rushing back they find within the gloom
the cloths and napkin empty as the tomb.
This Peter saw, and John, and they believed.

The Third Song of Magdalene

"My heart has
no lofty aims,
I am not concerned
with gains,
enough for me
in keeping my soul tranquil.
My delight
to follow Thee,
with my brothers
happily,
like a child
whose faithfulness is simple.

You who listened
to my prayer,
let me offer
you my care,
praise you with
the gift of my resources.
This is how
your servant serves,
nourished by
your ways and words,
finding rest in you,
my strength, my fortress."

One day under
heavy skies,
with His mother
at her side,
she endured
the sorrow of conviction.

Seeking strength
in their embrace,
these two Marys
came to taste
the bitterness
of living crucifixion.

Pondering
the hours and days
leading to this hill
she stayed,
helping to remove
His broken body.
Then she knew
whom she had sought
satisfied
her hungry heart,
taught her to believe
is being worthy.

Faithful
to her Lord in life,
Mary walked
with Him in strife,
sought Him in
the tomb of desolation.
First to witness
and proclaim
in the power
of His name,
without the grave
there is no resurrection!

Nightfall

Are these but shadows cast by candlelight
or images of darkness cast by men?
Day fails, the evening comes and once again

the terrors of uncertainty and night
prey on men the fear to breathe, and worse,
a prospect they had never known before,
that this could be the night that ends the world.
Hope expiring in a prison hearse.

Suddenly stood Jesus in their midst!
Holding forth His hands He smiled and said,
"Peace be with you," and another dread
struck their fragile courage like a fist.
"Peace be with you," Jesus did repeat.
"Why are you agitated? Why these doubts?"
Held in fright no answer could be found
until He asked them for something to eat.

And after this He breathed on them and said,
"Receive the Holy Spirit," then was gone.
But Thomas who was absent came along
demanding proof that Jesus wasn't dead.
Doubt tormented Thomas until he
was standing in the presence of the Lord.
With his hands inside His wounds, these words,
"Blessed is he who believes yet does not see."

The Fourth Song of Magdalene

In the upper
chamber where
bound by
unity of prayer
Mary found regard
from the Apostles.
Wounded by
humility,
now she understood
that she
bore what they desired
to be faithful.

42

Pondering
the days ahead,
to evangelize
or wed,
on her knees
in holy contemplation.
"Tell my, Lord,
your holy will,
Ephesus or
distant hills,
whither goest I
at your direction?"

As the Risen Lord
was seen
to favour
Mary Magdalene,
lifting her above
doubt and despairing.
And her sorrows
taken flight,
and her soul
filled with delight,
like a child
she went away rejoicing.

Daybreak

The death of Jesus and its aftermath,
darkness, lightning, anger from the land,
worried Cleopas and his troubled friend
plodding west along a dangerous path.
A stranger joined their weary stride and said
all these matters had long been ordained,
and going through the prophets he explained.
But they were blind until He broke the bread.

Later Jesus showed Himself again.
Watching from the shore He told them, "Try
casting your nets on the other side,"
and Peter jumped into the sea and swam.
At last He took them out to Bethany
where, as He gave His blessing, the eleven
saw their Lord ascending into heaven
and they worshipped Him on bended knee.

These men of Galilee went full of joy
back into the temple there to praise
God continually until the day
He clothed them with the power from on high.
One disciple vouched all these things true
and wrote them in a book for you and me.
That we whose eyes are open may yet see
His reign of peace and all the world renewed.

———————————

Above you see the Lord arise
to hold you precious in His sight.
Around you see the glory shine,
His glorious everlasting light.

Fastings

Sometimes during the day
you reach the critical point.
Light-headed as a blown dandelion,
your stomach becomes a fist clenched;
when relaxed, released emptiness
groans like a bellowing leviathan.
You drink a cup of water to send him away.
His imagined bulk spasms in garrulous complaint.
Above this journey of nothingness
heartbeats parley the terms of surrender.
Over and over and over you hear
them murmur and whisper the easy way out;
your age, your health, your weakness.
Escape clauses for the vincible.

At Gethsemane You prayed.
When the Father prepared to anoint
You for the sacrifice, three times
You implored His providence.
In your sadness and distress,
three times the sorrowful lamentation;
"If You are willing, take this cup away.
But if I must drink of it, give me strength."
Then cunning Satan put you to the test
offering himself as your deliverer;
Your friends sleep. He doesn't care.
You are weak. You suffer. You doubt.
Abandon this foolish pettiness.
Temptations for the untemptable.

Expectations

At last it has arrived,
a perfect day.
If it could be described
I think I'd say
something about the sky's
Madonna blue,
or failing that, I'd try
relating you
the feelings that arise
as if this new
day was the first day
and I in Eden,
but fail.

For how can one see with
the eyes of God?
All I can do is sit
with paper pad
and pen and wait for words
that never come.
And yes, it is absurd
to gaze upon
an empty page as if
words would appear.
They don't.

Last night He blessed me
with a three-fold dream.
A soul-embracing light
fell like a beam
dissolving flesh and blood and bones
to warmth and peace and joy
which I became.
"Such happiness!" I cried. "I want to be
like this forevermore!"
Thrice came the light, each visit
thrice more rapturous than before.

Then, like a jolt, the sudden
light of morning, grey and cold.
The years have dimmed this
whisper sent from heaven to a soul.
Lately troubles aggravate my heart,
flesh and blood and bone
succumb to sin and my world falls apart.
But then, a most amazing thing!
My son, my unassuming son
responding to another loud despair;
"It's not so much to worry
as to persevere."

The Candle

Old Father McCarthy's hair
was whiter than brilliant snow
but he walked with
spring in his step.
His sharp eyes and
quicker wit took advantage
of an irregularity on the altar
this morning; one of the
candles was out.

I stood against the wall
rocking on my heels
surveying the thousand or more
students shepherded into
St. John the Baptist Church
for Advent services.
One blond boy had tied
his long hair with a yellow elastic
in a fashion which reminded me
of our first born.
When he arrived nearly
twenty two years ago,
we were delighted!
Surely the sun
had finally found purposes
for rising!

"As we prepare to celebrate
this Mass," he was saying,
"I thank you for your silence."
And by God, they were!
The old priest said nothing
they hadn't heard from others,
but they listened to him.

Brendan was the light
of our eyes from the start.
Everyone in the world must know
that he was the most beautiful
baby ever born.
We didn't walk with him those days,
we floated on the bright summer air.
In the evening he was
the only star in the firmament.
Even God knew that!
And then his light
started to fade.

The boy with the blond hair
put his hands into his pockets
during the hymns.
I fought to forgive him.

"Why do you suppose this
candle's out? He asked
knowing there'd be no reply.
"Why do you think he's out
while his brother over there
burns brightly?"
I didn't know where he
was leading but he had
me along with the pony tail
and all his friends.
He swept his searching eyes
like a great lighthouse beam penetrating
deeply into each living soul.
"Why?" he repeated
holding up his hands
to frame the
golden silence.

The blond boy looked
over and caught my eye.
He was thinking.
I could see it in his expression.
He turned back to
the saintly old man on the altar.
"I'll tell you why,"
he said moving towards
the empty glass container.
He waited.
We all waited in stillness.
Whatever he was about to say now
would burn forever into our memory,
for he had brought us
to a darkness against which
he held the lamp
and we were crying out
for enlightenment.

"If this candle could talk
it would say, 'I've gone out
because there's nothing
inside me to burn.
My friend is full
so he makes a bright flame.
I'm gone out because
I'm empty.
That's why'."

Father McCarthy
took a step forward
then pointed his right hand
directly at the boy in front of me.
"Do you have in you
the stuff to be
one candle
bringing light
into the world?"
I wanted to tell him
he wasn't the only one in the church
who felt a sudden chill
race along his spine
to seize his heart.

Thursday

The man on the kneeler
in front of me
smelled of work.
The skin of his hands looked
like bark roughened
from years of hewing or
shaping or splitting.
The air around him carried
the unmistakable sweet
heaviness of earth,
as if he had just
come in from a day of cutting turf
on the bog;
it was that fresh.
It was as fresh and sweet as
the smell from the chipper
they had used last week
when the tree removal crew
had felled our beloved maple,
whose massive trunk had split
when winter rainwater
jammed an ice chisel
into its heart.

The man on the kneeler
in front of me
was young but well
into manhood.
Except for the rising of his shoulders
with each breath,
he moved very little.
Bent over the back of the bench
and breathing slowly,
he might have been carrying
the weight of the world,
such was his stoop.
The lapels of his outdated
greatcoat were shiny
and thin and frayed
    from wear.
Perhaps he had been
carrying something after all,
or had slept in this blanket
turning up the collar
for more heat.
I couldn't see his shoes
but imagined they were very old
too and might even be
worn through.
Everything about him
seemed old, and yet he was not
an old man.

The man on the kneeler
in front of me
didn't move when we
got up to leave.
It was dark now and everyone
was leaving.
Only a few lit candles
kept the darkness from being total,
kept him visible to us as we
lingered by the door
wondering.
In the parking lot
we said no one had seen him before,
here or in the neighbourhood.
Someone decided he looked familiar
but couldn't be certain.
As for me, I had the sudden notion
that he could have been my brother
had I made the effort to look
at his face.
He certainly was somebody's son.
But it was cold and dark.
Clouds were blotting the stars
and I was cold.
I don't know who he is, I said.
Let's go home.

Aging

1

I am standing at this barn door
Of a window twenty feet up
Trying to find a metaphor
For snow lying along long thin
Branches of freeze-dried trees.

I am morning's man but something
Today is amiss. Behind my eyes
A roiling wave of nausea
Leaves me witless and cold as a frog.
Ambivalent. Slightly unsound.

I am my own dialogue
As in a dream half-remembered
At dawn when we long to retrieve,
Desperately probing the shroud
As the longed-for dissolves.

I am troubled in spirit and flesh;
The emotional weight of self-pity
Hangs like a heavy shawl
To un-slippered feet awash
In the two-fold chill enveloping me.

2

The two-fold chill
Of body and soul:

When cold leaches in
Through muscle and marrow
And skin becomes parchment
Mottled and sallow.

When tired means weary
From resting too much,
And aching for contact,
Bruise at the touch.

When after the glow
From the loving cup
We curse the pain
And the self-distrust.

When we gaze like a fool
At a buttonless blouse
Pretending a smile
Could ever arouse.

When fathers and daughters,
Mothers and sons
Fearfully dance
Around verbs and nouns.

When I and my fellow
Unlovable blight,
Are shuttered away
Out of mind, out of sight.

When language is shaped
Inclusive and sterile.
Meaningless. Politic.
Paradigm infantile.

When truth caves in
Like a house of cards.
Is facing extinction.
Is anathema.

When youthful exuberance
Blows off the lid,
Counters civility
As we once did.

When genders pervert
And babies become
"Persona-non-grata,"
The race has been run.

When I kneel before Him
Whose breath is life,
There is contention.
There is strife.

3

And as reason is drawn
Into the whirlpool of dread,
Things unknown
Retreat and later
Emerge in dreams
Only to disappear
Again. But questions persist
And what's most
On my mind is this:
Is wisdom endangered
By age? Having time
To think, to consider
That we are running
Out of time to think,
To consider the yin
And yang of it all
Is the humorous twist.
Affective. Cerebral.
And I wonder
What kind of wind
Blew me here,

Here to this place
On this planet
To this age
In God's unfathomable
Measure of time.
On the sliding scale
Of creation's wonders,
Snowflakes observed
Without metaphor
Should not distress,
They being unsolvable,
Perfect and peerless.
Unlike the failure
Of simple language
For snow on a tree
One winter day,
The problem's more philosophical;
It is a rope too short
Thrown to a drowning man
Just out of reach.
It is failure to define growing old,
The inevitable confrontation
Between body and soul.

4

Old men's dreams are madness and true.
The worshipping eyes of a woman in love.
Clenched fists at dawn. Darkness at noon.
Angels in chorus, in beautiful chorus.
The naked terror of warplanes above us.

Towering mountainous spheres of doom
Rolling across horizonless fields
Closer, closer, out of control,
All to be levelled. Everyone crushed.
Then of a sudden it stops. Inert.

As I talk to myself of torments and dreams,
My thoughts as flighty as birds in trees,
Imprudent as waltzing on wobbly knees,
I find it amusing and somewhat perverse
That I should write it out in a verse.

I dreamt of a moment where language fails
And I wished when I wakened to hold it again.
And I closed my eyes in search of remains.
And I try to remember. I try to remember.
I try to remember. I try to remember.

Solicitude

When you have come to the age
where you can say you are growing
out of your years, few remain,
having spent them on mundane
or lofty things, never knowing
for sure the measure of your worth,

Take stock and ask yourself this;
"If I have nothing to hide,
looking into the full-length mirror
of conscience and responsibility, however
heavy the reflection or blithe,
have I earned my mother's trust?"

She was always your mother,
never a child or girl or woman in bloom
as you once were childlike
and youthful and full of life.
She was always known and assumed,
and never grew old as you are now old.

If her image stood beside yours
as you remember her best,
the most beautiful woman alive,
rose-water fresh, soft-eyed,
casually strong, that lavender dress
she loved, what would she say?

In your imagined mirror you reach for her hand,
the suddenly stop. You have doubts.
You were always precious in her sight,
and she loved you, loved you in spite
of the overtime you put in calling out
for more and more and more.

But you claim a disclaimer, a default;
the ignorance of never having known
mothers grow old, imperceptibly, gradually,
entering that invisible country
until at lastly she found the great unknown
while you were inventing solicitude.

Go find a quiet, holy place
and find your knees and hide your face,
and look into your mother's heart,
and seek the ever shining star
abiding there, for there you are.

Proselyte

There was nothing more sanguine and startling
that ever appeared.
The surgeon's hand mending the womb;
out of the tear,
presumptuous and small as a grasshopper's leg
his fingers were there,
exploring the hovering hand.
Stopping his heart.

For his part,
no surge of flesh and blood,
the butchering act,
could ever happen again.
That innocuous technical irony,
womb become tomb,
cut out by the delicate stroke
of an axiom.

An obstinate incontestability.
Death's moratorium.
There was no room for philosophy here,
only extremities.
Flourishing flowers or falling leaves.
Only these.
Only the thrown wide open door.
And welling tears.

Those Who Watch And Wake And Weep

Now when I was a young man coming into my own,
I welcomed each day bright and eager.
With a wife and a house on the edge of a park
And a sparkling career as a teacher.
When I stood at the end of the month in the queue
Dreaming about all the things we could do,
For the money was massive in seventy-two,
Life was good. All was well. No mistaking.

      And I thank God for graces and blessings.
      For His shoulder in case I should fall.
      And I knew I should say,
      "Why don't you lead the way!"
      But I wanted control of it all.

I must have forgotten the bruises and scars
The uncertainty of the future.
The winters and summers of fifteen long years
Since I stepped off the boat like a stranger.
There was no going back. There was nowhere to go.
And nothing they told me could ever console
A boy who was frightened and spoke with a brogue,
The target of hard knocks and torment.

      And I should have asked God for his blessings.
      For His shoulder in case I should fall.
      But I couldn't say,
      "Why don't you lead the way!"
      My whole life seemed out of control.

The notion of being displaced wears you down
When the memory of homeland still lingers.
And whenever misfortune arrived at our door,
We packed up our trappings like tinkers.
Then one day my father forgot to come home,
My invalid mother collapsed at the blow,
And being the eldest of five helpless souls,
I enlisted myself in employment.

At the terminal yard where the trains turned around
There was always a job for a loader.
And when I grew tired of delivering the mail
I practised at being a soldier.
And there was the summer I'll never forget:
I was hired as a hustler in a carnival tent
Where I learned how to swindle, but have no regret
For those two weeks of smug retribution.

There's a price to be paid at the end of the day
Like a man who can't swim in deep water
Who thrashes and splashes and crashes about
'Till he finally succumbs and goes under.
So the books lay unopened, assignments undone,
Another term wasted, another year gone.
And I watched all my fellows succeed and move on
While clouds gathered on my horizon.

I cannot remember or maybe don't know
The how or the why or the moment,
But I passed the exam, and the same afternoon
Completed the forms for enrolment.
I read Shakespeare and Milton and W.B.,
Fine arts and music and philosophy,
And I cried out, "Hurrah!" when I framed my degree
And hammered it up on the wall.

And I should have thanked God for His blessings.
For His shoulder in case I should fall.
And I knew I should say,
"Why don't you lead the way!"
But I held control of it all.

Our family had grown, there's three boys and four girls
In a house that is more like a castle.
There's a few more credentials of various forms
And I have become a headmaster.
There's a car in the driveway, vacations are planned,
A red sky at sunset, tomorrow looks grand.
I heard somebody say, "He's a successful man!"
And who was I to dispute it?

The voice on the phone was anguished, distressed,
Was fumbling for words through the sighing.
"Your dad……. our father…… is dead," it announced
Then it broke and my brother was crying.
My head started spinning. He said, "Are you there?"
I gasped like a fish out of water for air.
In anger, in anger I started to swear
At this ultimate final betrayal.

My sister had sent him a Father's Day call
To patch up the past over dinner.
But he died on the eve from that terrible blow
When the heart beats its last blaze of temper.
And later that summer we started to mend,
Finding forgiveness, when the phone rang again.
A car crash had taken the life of a girl
Who sat in the desk by the door.

And I should have asked God for His comfort.
For His shoulder in case I should fall.
And I didn't say,
"Why don't you lead the way"
To the box in that death-curtained hall.

Where went the promise that time heals all wounds,
Like a melody soothing the savage?
While my wife was surviving a difficult term,
I was visited by a grim presage.
My body surrendered to chronic fatigue,
Another term ended, but I wasn't at ease.
And we needed a passage of undisturbed peace,
Not even a whisper of dread.

But that dark premonition arrived like a shot,
Too ugly, too soon, too unwelcome.
"…was travelling too fast…..impaired….gravel road,
Names withheld…..further investigation."
It was almost a year to the day since the last
Time we sat through the gloom of a funeral Mass.
She was only fifteen and she came from the class
That seemed to be under a curse.

At the place where the town line is crossed by a road
A church had been built by the farmers.
And after a while when they added the school
It became the community's heartland
Where the annual concert was such an event,
Where bake sales were parties and everyone went,
And when tragedy struck, the country folk wept
For the loss of one of their own.

Still we prayed and we hoped for a happier end
To another school year and the summer.
The parents, the families with whom we were friends,
Holding anxiously on to each other.
Then September arrived on the wave of a sigh
And I was transferred to a school closer by.
There was reason to look to the future with joy,
Until somebody knocked on our door.

It was twenty-four months since I last saw these girls
At that small country school graduation.
With their lipstick and perfume, their dresses and heels
They had taunted the boys to frustration.
"We'd like to come in. Can we stay a few days?"
My wife saw it first, saw the sorrow and pain.
As she held out her arms the youngest one said,
"We've each just had an abortion."

And I asked God for some explanation,
For His shoulder in case I should fall.
And I wanted to say,
"Didn't You lead the way?"
But I could say nothing at all.

At a moment like this one can only conclude
The asylum is run by the patients,
That the world has gone mad, that the devil has won
And that God has abandoned his station.
In a very short time we had witnessed the worst,
Two girls in two boxes lying broken and crushed,
Two little tarts trying to grow up too fast
And their babes vacuumed out of their wombs.

We found our composure and guided them home
Still shaken like they were our daughters.
We had given them words and rehearsed a scene
To explain to their fathers and mothers.
Whatever the outcome we never were told,
But Death stalked and added one more to his toll;
The youngest one died on a dark country road,
Thrown out of a tumbling car.

The loss of young lives is a terrible thing
Giving rise to unanswered questions.
With our own seven children, more precious, more loved,
We suffered alongside the parents.
I thought about choices and how we'd arrived
To encounter misfortune and learned to survive,
How we were not abandoned and never deprived
Of God and his merciful care.

My mother succumbed to a fatal disease
Shortly after my father's heart felled him.
And the carnage that bloodied the life of my school
Took place in the five years between them.
When I stood at the grave where her body would rest
A remarkable peace entered into my breast,
And I didn't feel angry and I wasn't lost.
And I thought I would like to go home.

      And I thanked God for graces and blessings.
      For His shoulder in case I should fall.
      And I'm learning to say,
      "Why don't you lead the way!"

Watch, dear Lord
with those who wake
or watch or weep tonight,
and give your angels charge
over those who sleep.
Tend your sick ones,
O Lord Jesus Christ,
rest your weary ones,
bless your dying ones,
soothe your suffering ones,
shield your joyous ones,
and all for your love's sake.
              St. Augustine.

Fault Line

Somewhere between dazzling
high season sunlight, retreat
into shadow, the optic nerve fails.
Like tectonic plates colliding
make the fragile earth vibrate
in unexpected pain,

it leave us blinded by darkness.
Where bright light and dark light
collide, there lies the fault
line of vision. At best
we stumble in uneven flight
from that which we sought,

prayed and wished to appear.
At worst, the familiar becomes
dangerous. We are immobilized
by fear and alarm. In here
we go groping and fumbling.
Out there, we are fully alive.

Light Through Leaves

1

It is a light and airy room,
the weeping fig leaves nary stir.
Mottled sunlight beams illume
a solitary soul at prayer.

There is a solemn stillness here
where dawn of day dismisses night
awakening the leafy bower
wrapping him in robe of light.

He prays, "O King who made the stars
who made the earth and fashioned me,
come and soothe my grieving heart
sadder than this weeping tree."

In robe of light the man became
his image beautiful and good,
for everything that God had made
He looked upon and called it good.

"I would like to have the men
of heaven who are heaven blest,
I would like to know again
in my own home their cheerfulness."

And when he saw the man recline
beside the tree of light and shade,
brought a woman to his side,
made them one and unashamed.

"As little stars they were and pure,
unashamed their innocence.
Nor were any holier
nor equal in their sinlessness."

For the sage; the rules of war
between the forces light and dark
are writ upon the fleeting air
by crooked hand of fallen star.

What goes before the fall but pride!
They looked into the bitter glass,
enchanted, lovestruck, starry-eyed
and fell from piety and grace.

As an angel he appeared
pleasing to the eye, with praise
he seduced their vanity
and swept their innocence away.

Thus it was they hid from God
and could not contemplate His face,
so fearful is their fearsome Lord,
so pitiful their nakedness.

2

Beautiful and good is all
that God created from a void.
Not from substance shape or form
but where will and "Be!" collide.

None there was and none shall be
who comprehends the heavenly plan.
Who entertains eternity.
Who ever did or ever can.

Think about the Holy Three
on the mountain's awful height,
turned their mortal eyes away.
Blinded by transfigured light.

Dare to look God in the face?
Look you first into the sun!
Still, man has his pride of place
and thinks himself as wonder-full.

He thinks, and thus he is divine,
wrapped in robe of self-delight,
searching God beyond the sky,
trifling with very life.

He peers into the starry night
through his glinting looking glass,
chasing the ineffable light
far beyond his mortal grasp.

Or with the angel of deceit
entreating falsely in his ear,
commits the ultimate conceit;
in his own images re-creates.

But when the sun and moon depart
the shadow of primeval fear
clouds the superstitious heart
and all bravado disappears.

For 'things that go bump in the night'
awake the slumberer's venerable dread,
unless he don the suit of light
and to his maker bow his head.

On righteous man and fallen man
like light through leaves His glory shines,
blessing him, provoking him,
in robe of light and weeping eye.

To every prayer God's ear is turned
His ear is turned to every slight,
and He will long forget the curse
and find in every prayer delight.

The measurement of man and leaves
their glory, sadness, rise and fall,
in seasons and in centuries
is fragile and ephemeral.

But when the earth has disappeared
the sun and moon and stars gone dim,
the holy city will appear
and He will be Emmanuel.

His truth shall be their cornerstone
and every nation become one
in glory that is God alone.
Not added to. Not taken from.

Listenings

If you want to hear
the sound of all that is,
the universe retreating,
anti-matter's hiss,

singing stars and gleaming
galaxies, planets near
and far humming round
their suns, the crystal clear

Aurora Borealis
chorusing and dancing
like painted veils of light,
cover your pyjamas

in hat and coat and glove,
step out after midnight
one winter's night so cold
the view is unimpeded,

look into the heavens,
let the moment swell,
listen to the silence
and wonder at its spell.

2

If you want to hear
the voice of the Creator
animating everything
before it came to be,

voweling the vastness,
codifying consonants,
issuing the future's
forever harmony,

coaxing light from darkness,
courting you with graces
sweet as morning rain,
patiently awaiting

the favour of your answer
a million million years.
Somewhere in between
sunrise and sunrise

close your eyes and listen
past the pandemonium,
the quiet invitation
whispered in your ear.

Sunday

It is the alpha and omega
of the week. The day God
rested from the work
of creation and rose to make
all things new.
Anathema
to all things servile.

Alpha and omega of salvation!
On the seventh day God rested,
His work of creation completed.
On this day in the watershed
of His bountiful mercy and grace,
we take leave of our servility
in our still and sunny place.

Bethlehem

A hell-fire fury wind comes from the North
to level in a blast the walls of stone
and fled afar the terrorized temple lambs.
And you, O shepherd Bethlehem, your worth
is naught this day. This hour, you are alone.
You sent them from you to Jerusalem,
innocent, unblemished, babes of Spring,
new life flourishing a wilderness
like promised hope that comes with every dawn.
They took your lambs to expiate their sin.
O Bethlehem, they paid a king's distress.
But the North wind cries for you and your first born
The Lamb of God you cradled from crib to cross.

Mother Mary

I was dreaming of my mother in my little childish way,
how to tell her that I love her using words I cannot say.
Does she feel me when I'm moving? Can she hear me
    when I sigh?
Does the whisper of my heartbeat light her face with
    tender pride?

I was searching for my mother when I'd finished all my
    play.
I was tired and bruised and hungry and had used up all the
    day.
I called and called and called her holding back the fear
    inside,
then I saw her by the roses and her arms were open wide.

I was longing for my mother for my life had gone astray.
I had learned to count my blessing but forgotten how to
    pray.
Would she know me now? I wondered if her love for me
    had died,
then I found her in the Rosary kneeling closely by my side.

Nightwatch

These hills of my ancestors,
David's delight,
wrap like a blanket
around me this night.
I can see in the distance
the flickering light
of the fires of my fellows,
the fires of my people,
enflaming our hearts.
All is well. All is right.
For unto us,
said the prophets of old,
in my humble village
this deep night and cold,
a king for all nations
on earth to behold,
is born to a maiden
in that little stable
where shepherds and angels
their praises are told.

And He will shepherd
all men of good will,
burning his love
on their hearts like a seal,
call on His children
of light to be still,
to be humble and little
like a lamb in a stable,
and fear not the shadows
that stir in the hills.

The Misunderstanding Of Power

Someone had used a roll of tape
to put a line of marks
across the floor where they would stand.
Like predatory sharks,
these gentlemen in blue suits
smiled polished smiles into
the polished TV camera lens
seducing you and me.

Those exchanging whispered notes,
one on the left, one right,
are the principals of power.
They are the men of might
who hold our lives like so much sand.
That diplomatic touch
proffers the other to the mic,
so little means so much.

I watch them at their childish games,
the rituals of state
performed beneath the glassy dome
where treachery and hate,
their true agendas lurk behind
each calculated word.
This is the theatre someone once
referred to as absurd.

What do men know who wave their hands
in posture for the press,
who speak in silver platitudes
and beat upon their breast?
How could they know, these men whose actions
shape the world's design,
that God is in my flower garden
playing with my child?

Angels
of creation

God who is Love who is God
who is Love without restraint,
discharged across His heavenly court
divine sparks of his own Self.
These angelic beings love
Him whose love loves all He made
and they serve Him who is Love
and He loves whom He creates.

God gathered clamour and chaos.
Into his mighty hands He drew
and charged with vitality all
things. Everything, everything new
He commanded them "Be!" and "Amen."
To his angels were assigned grace,
duties and powers given them
according to favour and place.

To some were given the fruitful earth
and all its givingness. To others
the wandering winds and their vaults.
The seas, the fountains of water,
shaping and consuming fire
to angels belong. The elements
of creation, lower and higher,
obey the spirits Yahweh sent.

They gather birds to chorus sunrise.
Every day the first reborn
in songs, delight, conceived surprise.
Oh, glorious, glorious eastern morn!
Angelic light igniting life
in angelic exhilaration,
life angelic igniting light
in mirth-loving expectation.

Or heaving heavy hoary seas,
or savage ruinous tempest sent,
or frigid winter's endless freeze,
or sun-scorched earth temperament,
these marvels are to angels charged
in the government of God
as they propagate and purge
in concert with God who is love.

of appointment

God called His great Archangels
as by their names. "Stand before
the glory of my throne. Raphael,
my sunlight, my healing power.
Tell my children how to seek
my blessings and mercy, say
to them my mercy's reach
extends beyond the power of prayer.

"Phanuel and Uriel
search the corners of the world,
stand before my throne and tell
where the evil forces move.
Raguel bear my forgiveness
to sinners who call my name,
and Jophiel be the reflection
of my beauty eternal.

"Gabriel, great mediator,
speak my voice when I command,
and Michael Israel's mighty shepherd,
be the sword at my right hand.
Seraphim come stand before me
servants to my heavenly court.
Cherubim, your guardian duties
show my presence to the earth."

of rebellion

Thus it was until a great
dark unrest beset God's words.
Love who is God knew the pain
of rejection of his love.
Semhazah and Asael
and Lucifer demanded more;
not for them to love and serve,
so they waged a might war.

 As the enemies of God
warred against their maker Lord,
those who loved Love bravely fought
those who coveted his throne.
"Who is like God?" Michael cried
as he drove them in disgrace
sent them by his fiery sword
to the pit of endless flames.

Now Gadreel the fallen cursed
God and waited for a chance
in the garden where the first
man and woman were entranced
at the tree forbidden them.
He entreated them to doubt
God's commandment and intent
and they sinned and were cast out.

In the anguish of their loss
Eve and Adam grieved their fate
and like repentant children, sought
to re-enter Eden's gate.
But God sent a tower of flame
alongside cherub angel guards.
Until the fullness of time came
Heaven would be closed to all.

of confrontation

As a tiger lies in wait
Semhazah pounced at his chance
burning to his core with hate,
spurred by his own arrogance
and the mortal weaknesses
of humankind, in intercourse
he spawned an evil giant race,
and the vengeance of God's sword.

Asel's subtle craftiness
tempted mankind's baser depths;
he spoke to man's self-centredness
with wondrous instruments of death.
To women sly seductions gave,
clothed in jewels, scented skin,
purring promises, arrays
of lovely lustful wanton sin.

To the sons of God is given
long before he draws first breath,
an angel guide assigned from heaven,
defender, guardian advocate.
He to help him overcome
temptations, weakness of the flesh,
nudge him gently, help him learn
the holy path of righteousness.

Still the hearts of men turn cold
who laugh into God's holy face,
sell their souls for pagan gold
into the fallen angels' debt.
Philosophies make right of sin,
love gives way to fear and doubt
and the light of truth is dimmed,
and armies draw their swords and shout.

Lines are drawn, curses cursed
in the name of God, in his
sacred name human worth
and life summarily dismissed
or swept away like burning grass
and justified by reason's lies.
This is the devil's merry dance.
This is why the angels cry.

of salvation

God who is Love who is God
sent Gabriel to woe a maid
most loved by God who is Love
and this is what Gabriel said;
"God's favour upon you is high
you who will bring forth His Son."
Then he paused for her reply,
and Mary said, "God's will be done."

While he slept Joseph encountered
Gabriel stirring in his dreams
and the angel asserted,
"You have responsibilities."
Joseph took Mary in marriage
and honoured her virginal womb.
and being of David's lineage,
fulfilled the prophetic amen.

How sweetly did the angels sing
a thousand thousand voices raise
glories to the newborn king,
alleluias, songs of praise
when Mary's Jesus Christ was born
under heaven's happiness,
in that simple bed of straw,
the humblest heir of kingliness?

Again Joseph met the angel
like a torment in a dream
with a sobering instruction
for his holy family.
"Go to Egypt," said the angel,
"And when the evil king is dead,
bring your family to Nazareth."
And Joseph did what the angel said.

Angels watched the Son of God
take on our humanity.
He who trod where angels trod,
walked with men who disbelieved.
How the Father's heart was torn
when his Son was crucified
like a common criminal
on a dark cold mountainside.

But he raised him from the grave
in fulfilment of the plan
of salvation. We were saved
by his resurrection and
it was an angel who rolled back
the tomb's great and heavy door,
and the clutching hands of death
are empty now and evermore.

of amazement

Angels cherish us their cousins
slightly less than wondrous made.
They plead for us when in trouble,
cheer for every debt repaid,
grieve with us, rejoice with us,
salve the bruises of our soul,
laugh with us (Oh! How they laugh!),
laugh at us a thousandfold.

At the sacred sacred moment
to the sacred altar stone,
God, Almighty God is summoned
by His priest and He must come.
Angels kneel beside his vestments,
holy angels watch in awe,
hear a mortal's soft pronouncement
summon God as they cannot.

Angels are not far beyond us
as we might believe they are.
Sent to us by Love who loves us
they are closer than the stars.
Sometimes angels come before
as strangers knocking on our door,
and to strangers, being kind,
we draw angels to our side.

of conceit

From the shadows of tomorrow
creeps the god-like bestial man
radiating self-made glory,
"Who has seen such as I am?
I have swept across the heavens,
left my mark on distant spheres.
In my likeness of an angel,
who is there that I should fear?"

Finding Joseph

Oh where, oh where is our daughter Mary?
Oh where, oh where can our Mary be?
She is yonder talking to the man named Joseph
in the olive garden by the crooked tree.

And how is Joseph prepared to bring them
to the town of David by Caesar's decree?
For his wife and babe he has found a donkey
and she will ride on and he will lead.

Oh why are Mary and her son crying?
What is the sadness their hearts must own?
They have lost their husband and father Joseph
who has been called to his heavenly home.

And what is Joseph to this poor country?
And what is Joseph to me and you?
He is counsel for a happy dying
and patron saint for this country too.

And when can we encounter Joseph?
And who will lead us nearer still?
Mary and Jesus will bring us closer
and he will answer when we call on him.

Camino Sketches

I   The Plan

All the arrangements had been made
months before on the internet.
"Because we're old," Estelle had said
we six would meet at Sarria
for the final leg. The easy days.

Months before, a ten day stroll
to the tomb of St. James, a holy
journey for pilgrims I told
myself, meant Rosary beads dangling
from one hand, a walking pole

in the other. Alleluias, Praises Be
and Glorias. Not for the faint
of spirit. Maybe not for me.
Sarria. Michael and I drove
two cars to the first Albergue,

brought one back and strode out
to catch the others half-an-hour
ahead. We would go about
this arrangement to Santiago
leapfrogging the Spanish route.

II   Setting out

They say that kings
and princes had walked
The Way. That Dante
had struggled up

this wooded brow,
had gasped for breath
reaching the top
as I did now.

A robin darted
among eucalyptus leaves
singing her clarion
song whenever she stopped.

Then she would wait
for me to pass
and like a child
wanting someone to play,

repeatedly fly on
ahead. But never away.
This little bird, thought I,
is cheeky and cruel,

is mocking my light-headed
pause as her ancestors
had before to saints
and scholars and fools.

I nodded my head to her
and resumed the road.

A vision fell into step
Like a half remembered dream.
A field of furze,
two blood-thirsty boys

crawling around with clubs
to murder a bird,
carry him door-to-door
for a penny to bury the wren.

Pockets heavy with coins
to buy sweets, the body
was dumped in a ditch
without guilt. The perfect crime.

If I closed my eyes
in regret over life or death,
the uneven weight
of the pack would do me in.

I angled my body
for balance and gait,
gathered my wits and dismissed
the ghosts of youth.

The heat of the day
was mounting now.
The woods became still.
And no birds sang.

III   Encounters

Sunday morning. Next stop Portomarin,
an impossible distance for midday Mass
and age-weary legs to achieve.

Una said John without Mass would distress,
might not believe that God would forgive
a soul for doing its best.

Santa Maria de Ferreros, a small stone church
Locked. Two women replacing
faded flowers with crest at an ancient cross.

They worked with practised purpose
at their task, utterly void of cheer.
Cheerless faded aprons matching

colourless scarves around faces grim and austere.
I thought we were watching
a ritualistic lament,

as if the cold of the lifeless stone
always insinuating itself
always with patient intent

year after year had finally broken the will
to find joy in the task.
And maybe voyeurs are judging them still.

Two gunshots too close for comfort for me
shattered the morning air.
I rounded a corner in time to see

him make an appearance as casual as an old cat.
There was something almost natural
in the drape of the gun on his back.

Then the car, the trailer, the barking dogs.
A pair of blood-thirsty curs
and me, tremblings and doubts.

When he silenced the engine and headed off somewhere,
the dogs turned it up a notch
and we might have moved from there

had not someone opened the church and gone inside.
It was a travelling priest,
dogs and clatter and bangs taken in stride.

As John encouraged us out of this strange tableau
we obeyed. The Mass,
in Spanish spoken and sung, unknotted our souls.

IV   Slogging

Linda was dangerously unprepared.
The mere ordinariness of taking a walk
on quiet streets translated here
inversely. After the third day
encouraged by me and the Spanish air,
she challenged The Way's authority.

El Camino is travelled alone.
It can be a private Calvary,
struggling over slick bedstones
or wet Galician clay, bent
under the shifting back-biting load.

It can be a private Calvary,
as the creeping frailty of old limbs
imposes itself into each stride,
gathering calf-cords, tauting shins.
Inventing blisters secretively.

It can be a private Calvary
when you promise violent heart and lungs
a reprieve from the toils, a ridge achieved,
and all you can do is drop your shoulders, curse
a whispered curse at one more cursed scree.

It can be a private Calvary.
Winding sun-scrubbed flinty corridors
where every spawning Celsius degree
gives rise to waves of sweat across your back,
and "Agua, por favor," your shameless plea.

It can be a private Calvary:
a sudden blow! "What am I doing here?
I want to love the forest, but the trees…"
Brain-dried. Soul-sapped. Stood vertiginous.
"Where are you Lord. What do you want of me?"

V   A Bridge

There is a bridge at Portomarin
three hundred metres hip to hip

and half as high from head to heel.
Along the sides a walking slip.

Perigrinos stood around
El Camino mileage signs

for a picture. Even now
I experience butterflies

at the memory and the dread
of the steps I had to take.

Photos finished, I instead
of stalling, stalling, had to make

a decision which I did.
I stepped out to the yellow line

along the centre of the bridge
and told myself I would be fine.

Two or three times I looked back
to gauge the distance I had come.

My legs were wobbly, my stomach
tight and hollow as a drum.

I felt no victory when I came
to the other side. I knew

the only way I could reclaim
my senses was to continue

well beyond 'till I could see
the monster hadn't followed me.

VI   Peregrinos

Ruth sidled in beside us. Courteous stealth;
she simply arrived, adjusted to our stride
and wanting to explain matters as if
she was compelled to justify herself
for not walking with us all the time
suddenly shoot from the hip.
"I'm from Vancouver. Until I came
here I never carried a back pack.
A little further back I climbed a hill.
I'm seventy. I have only myself to blame.
Rested on a mossy stone, leaned back
and slid to the bottom. What a thrill!
Being rescued by those brawny lads, I mean!"

There is an understood rule on the trail;
walkers have right of way. When coming from
behind bikers must shout or ring a bell
according to a shaky sliding scale
of distance, time, weather and the unknown
frame of mind or riders and their wheels.
The girl from Amsterdam wanted to talk.
"One morning I got up, opened the door,
said goodbye and rode my bike away.
I have no regrets. I have not looked back."
She lied. Neither her heavy accent nor
her blue-eyed smile could cover the pain.
"Since then I've just been trying to find my way."

When George caught up with me I was worn out
from the heat of the day. "Buon Camino."
"Buon Camino," I answered hoping he
would pass and leave me to go about
my solitary self-pity. "You know
I'm not sure why I'm here," he said to me
then went silent for a longish spell.
"I'm an architect. Swiss. No one hires
an architect when there's a recession."
His voice quick and clear as a cow bell.
I credited his words with a weak smile.
And saying nothing more he carried on
outdistancing my wretchedness. Gone.

We came upon an angel sent by God
in answer to a prayer hours away
from our next stop. "Agua, por favor."
She heard the words, but more she understood
our plight. As if to say, "Don't be afraid,"
she beckoned us to her Casita door.
The yard enclosed a thousand years of peace;
three dozing dogs, a broken loaf of bread,
beside a wooden trough her ancient chair.
She praised God by her humble modesty,
the way she shied her eyes, lowered her head.
She gave us water wishing us to stay,
and as we left blew kisses through the air.

VII   A question

I joined the winding queue
to catch a glimpse
of St. James casket
in the Basilica's womb.

The line took on
a life of its own,
shoulder-to-shoulder
shuffling humanity

permitted a few seconds
to look then shunted
along to the end
of the tour.

It was the same
at Lourdes. A silent
winding shunting train
of gawkers hoping

this proximity to a
holy place would
somehow make us holier.
Maybe even saintlier.

Tick from the list
of holy places
I want to visit:
Knock, Lourdes,

Santiago de Compostella.
There are half-a-dozen
more but I am
no longer sure.

Have I disappointed God
in my unimpressedness?
Become less holier
a man?

VIII   An answer

We who have walked the Long Walk
a fragment or in its entirety
cannot remain unchanged or talk
about it in the abstract.

I am, at least, more inclined
towards a human company
soldiering the centuries
to win the holiest of shrines.

I have imagined the saints to life,
looked upon their countenance
seeking heaven in their eyes
along Iago's Camino.

I've even thought of going back
were it solely up to me.
The saints' heads were never haloed,
hands not always joined in prayer,

kinder to children and the poor.
I think they simply loved God more
than themselves. And who can say
we were not journeying with saints

step after step after step after step,
rising, falling, stressed, unstressed?
Loving it all in the present tense
proved a holy nourishment

as miracled as bread and fish,
as rich a blessing one could wish,
as a passage full of grace.
As welcome as a sacrament.

Morning In July

There's a perfect sky
and the air is clean,
washed over by last evening's storm.
The cat sleeps under
broad Hosta leaves
and the morning is blue and green and warm.

I think as I write
of a trusted friend
returning a folder of verse.
His simple appraisal
that I was compelled
to favour an economy of words.

A familiar squirrel
races over the lawn
scampering as fast up a tree.
Secure in his world
he hurls curses upon
the invasive impudence of me.

I am caught in the space
between moment and time;
the conflict of impulse and muse
unsettles the peace
and the natural rhyme
of season and solitude and mood.
To summon command
of my thoughts and words
is as easy as snaring a sigh.
Ah, but where there's a truth
in a phrase I have turned,
there too is a modicum of joy.

The clatter of tin
on the concrete path
announces a boy and his pal
taking the measure
of this and that
as they sport in the kicking of a can.

Unaware of my gaze
and the spell they cast,
they halt in mouth wide trace,
point at the branches
in silence, then laugh
resurrecting their early morning dance.

When I ponder these fleeting
encounters I find
there's a kind of cohesion they bring.
It's as if all creation
was shaped and designed
to accomplish such transitory things.

Then the squirrel and the boys
and these hodgepodge lines
might be thoughts in the mind of God,
whose love animates
and is filtered so fine
that nothing of value can be lost.

But if I should fail
at the end of the day
to proclaim what is good and wise,
I wonder if heaven
might soon slip away
like Adam's last glimpse of paradise.

A Sprig Of Flowers

How do we measure time?
We turn the wheel that
turns the spring that sets
the pendulum to swing
accumulating little things;
thoughts and heartbeats,
fluttering wings, thunder,
lightening, lovers' glances,
marathons for racers, dancers,
transatlantic business flights,
separating dark from light.
The period of a workman's wages,
gods and planets, lunar stages,
birth to dying, generations
rising, falling, empires, nations.

How do we measure time?
We print the page that
makes the book that gives
events a sterile look,
dehumanizing crown and crook.
The noble Golden Age of Greece,
a world engulfed in Roman peace.
Cities rise to be destroyed,
a carpenter is crucified,
Jerusalem invites Crusades,
Europe falls beneath the Plague.
Heads must roll in revolutions,
pacifists flee persecution.
Death comes falling from the sky,
a flash and half a million die.

How do we measure time?
We glorify, we idolize,
we gaze into another's eyes
drowned in a sea of heavy sighs.
Wishing the perfect human form
assured that Venus is reborn
under that designer dress,
this subtle rouge and sculpted tress.
We swear by witnessed ceremony
pagan, civilized or holy,
to be faithful ever after,
yours the tears, mine the laughter.
'Till tragically it bears fruition,
envy, jealousy, suspicion.

How do we measure love?
In songs and sonnets, words in rhyme,
deeds that lead the heart to pine,
flung in the face of unmoved time.

Did they conspire to kill the king
who was Pharaoh of the Nile,
because his views of God disrupted
policies of state, corrupted
by men who had too much to gain?
And when his widow in her pain,
placed the flowers on his breast
to sweeten his eternal rest,
did not she know this small bouquet
would love outlive and time decay?

Endtimes

No political
point of view,
no pulsating poetry
old or new,
no speech from the throne
left, centre of right,
bombastic platform,
reform plebiscite,
radio newscasts,
newspapers too,
reworded, reduced
by a classified censor
presenting a sterilized
point of view.

No bank of whatever
CEO,
market investor,
portfolio
manager, president,
fortune diviner,
lender of mortgages,
unsound debentures.

Passion filled mobs,
summer parades,
bawdy obscenities
shameless, unscrupulous
prancing and dancing
immoral charade.

No terrified soldier
with bayonet fixed,
no little red book,
no wild anarchist.
No emblems or flags,
no border invaders,
nor placards or tags
for forceful dissuader,

suicide bombers,
holy jihad
terrorist factions,
kidnappers, extortionists,
raging and howling
intensively mad.
No dishonourable
honourable men
smiling, conniving
for personal gain,
wheelers and dealers
of confidence winks,
secretive handshakes
and other dark tricks.

Spinners of zodiacs,
readers of palms,
stargazing tellers
of fame and calamity,
crystal ball soothsayers
selling their charms.

No human rights jesters,
no killer of babies,
no same gender hustlers
lobbying lies.
Aggressive proclaimers
of brave new worldliness,
tree-hugging, rose-sniffing
doers of goodliness,
cat lovers, dog lovers,
seafaring whale savers,
founders of movements
to save us from harm.
Pot heads, crack heads,
sniffers of glue,
traffickers lurking
in hallways and alleyways
peddling death
for a dollar or two.

No uninspired preacher
or misinformed teacher
prattling on about who
knows what.
Front door evangelists,
buy now pay laterists,
selling salvation and dreams
while they're hot.

Not even oil merchant
billionaires, trillionaires,
limousine chauffeured,
entourage pampered,
private jet, globe trotting
princes and sheiks.
Grocery store cart pushers,
no fixed address owners
sleeping on concrete beds,
poking through garbage bags,
clinging to life
by the skin of their teeth.

No chosen society
of illuminati
wickedly weaving a web
of deceit.
Democrat, communist,
liberal, conservative,
progressive, regressive,
positioned deadbeat.
Environmental activists,
space walking astronauts,
survivors of yet-to-be-fought
nuclear holocausts,
disheveled eccentric
celebrity scientists,
writers of warnings,
novelists, essayists.

No cleavage exposing
hourglass movie stars,
sexiest man in the world
or beyond,
no nay-sayers, yea-sayers,
Noble Prize laureates,
street walking hookers,
their pimps and their johns.

None of the following:
cyber apologists,
programmers, hackers,
networkers, gurus,
micro-chip processors,
futurists, spurious
prophets of self renewed
global recovery.
Not the haves nor the have-nots
the polarized classes,
the babbling crew
of this rudderless ark,
no behaviour or utterance
(I'm back where I started)
can evade or forestall
God's direful justice.

There was a cold hard rain today,
then the clouds broke.
Afterwards the singing of birds
and a rainbow.

Irises

At my feet where I sit,
a bold clutch of blue Irises.
Four and twenty blooms,
delicate and strong,
on strong green stems
amid the mob-like
urgent press of swords.
May my children's children's children
stand anew like these
in days to come,
delicate and strong
on strong green stems
amid the fern like
foliage of Spring.

Talk Show

"If you listen much longer to that, you know
it will drive you crazy," she warned.
Obediently I turned off the radio
and buried my head in the sand.
Where was the crime for being upset?
The matters that get my blood up
collide between life and death
and this morning I was in the mood.

Somewhere in the middle of middle decades
I had become indifferent and lost
sight of responsibilities. I was floating in the parade
with the rest, looking ahead to the point
in the road where the mortgage paid,
debt free, grandchildren giggling on my knee
comforts of life awaited.
I heard them call this posture 'cocooning.'
But the current and clamour and discord
flooded the dream like a torrent in Spring
and I suddenly knew there was work
to be done.

I became eighteen again. Visionary, passionate,
out to change the world. Mobilized and compelling.
Getting things done. Moxie unlimited. Activist.
There were letters to write, stories to tell,
meetings to attend, assist, organize. Prayer groups
emerged for monthly huddles at somebody's house.
The word got around. Support groups
arrive to engage, reinforce.
Soon we were a mob,
empowered with righteous commission,
patting ourselves on the back for a job
well done. Out of control with holy discretion.
Floating along.

I am confounded by the growing
preponderance of mankind divine.
Herc in the helter-skelter uproar
of twenty first century life, we look and find
in the mirror, God gazing back.
We have catalogued his supreme franchise
and want it for ourselves* as a matter of fact.
(*save for the marginalized).
Yes, the radio shook me up.

"I respect my listeners who are guided
by their religious beliefs and rules,
but let's put faith and law aside,"
he said. "What does your heart tell you?
What do your feelings say?
Should euthanasia be legalized
in this country today?"
A flood of callers, heroic and wise
as a biblical king chorused in:
        "We put down our pets when they're old."
        "Why should anyone die in pain?"
        "We can give them a dignified death?"
        "If they're unable to have a quality life,
        its what they would want."
        "We're not doing this for us, but for them."
        "It's not really killing, it's an act of mercy."
The affable host was pleased.
There was no debate. The door was opened
a little bit wider. There were possibilities.

I said to myself, here we go again!
It started this way in the sixties.
A word introduced in the public square
moved quickly from conversational east
to a law struck down and the cradle left bare.
Thus began the civilized slaughter of innocence
and from the basement of the womb,
millions of silent screams, sans acquiescence,

were torn from their living wombs.
Twice silenced. Twice sinned.
And what if they should have survived?
Being born has long term risks. Listening
to talk shows today I hear tomorrow prescribed
by the new avant-guardians of life.
I have broken from the crowd,
abandoned the comfortable drift
and discovered my own battle ground
lies under my feet. Family and friends
and like-minded people understand this;
from beginning of life to its end,
nothing transcends evil more than witness.

St. Jacob's Market

If you're visiting Wellesley someday,
give us a call and we'll take you
for a short drive East,
say, about twenty minutes or so,
and make our way
to the market at St. Jacob's.
It's best to go
in the Spring,
on a warm Spring morning
when a soft shower is rinsing
the white-brown snow,
and corn stalks
from last year's crop
stubble the fields.
The route winds through Mennonite farms
recalling old customs
and certainties
among wireless homes and barns,
the horse-worked land,
and black-robed children
in whitewashed schools.
We'll likely have to pass
slow moving buggies and walkers,
giving wide berth,
while craning our necks
to catch a glimpse
of these guardians of the land
before rushing on.
With luck, the rain
will have gone by now
and a burst of April sunshine
splash over all we survey,
like a moment of gladness
dispels an hour of gloom.
Then, around the bend,
the sudden sight of the market

spreading like a visiting carnival
that arrived at night;
a familiar mystery
that beckons us in.
And Oh, the market! The market!
You'll find your senses
awakened at every turn.
The air is imbued with
the fragrance of Spring in bloom.
Everywhere there are
sweet savouries and
fresh foodstuffs to sample.
Fruit and vegetables from vine
and branch spread over
acres of grounds,
with colourful fabric and garment
stalls giving frame to the place.
For us, the regular patrons,
it's another home among friends.
For you it'll probably be
an overwhelming delight,
a maze of enchantment that invites
a thorough explore.
You may stay all day if you want,
but just before you leave,
lingering in the cool shade of evening,
pause a little to listen to
the whisper of distant voices.

Spring Bees

Spring bees are no less
busy than those of Autumn.
It seems they never rest.
Wherever they come
from and where they go

is a mystery to me.
It's easier to follow
their communal industry
as they hover and dart and fly
from bluebell to crocus to violet

not knowing bees can't fly.
And if one should get
in the way of another,
a little "Excuse me," suffices
instead of "Don't bother

me, pal or you'll pay the price!
I've got a job to do
for my boss so buzz off
if you know what's good for you!"
But "Excuse me" is probably enough.

And the blossoms always accommodate
their insect intruders. Ever so gently
they bend with their weight
as if nodding politely
for services rendered before they withdraw.

Bees can make only so many visits
to a flower before all
its pollen is gone. When it's
empty, however, they continue to search
hoping to find the last

tiny grain missed by the rest.
They are past
caring about looking foolish
in this little failure,
for the next one might be as full as they wish.

I don't think it ever occurs
to Spring bees to be pests.
They are bigger and bolder
in Autumn, as I can attest,
and maybe because they are older,

good manners and patience are
in short supply like the hours
of sunlight and warmth. Far
be it from me to judge a bee, I'm no Spring flower.
But I know from past

experience that one need not fear
these pliers of blossoms in May. The last
time I was stung was late in the year.
Besides, I like watching these
happy visitors. One can learn a lot from bees.

Summer Bees

The woods are in their Summer splendour,
the nearby meadow blooms,
the swish of our strides is the only sound
 disturbing the afternoon.
On the sills of the hives we are startled to see
dead and dying bees.

There is plentiful fruit on hazel and beech.
The black and yellowing heads
of acres and acres of sunflower fields
witness the terrible dread,
the scattered casualties under the trees
of dead and dying bees.

The beekeeper's hope that this place was beyond
the reach of industrious man
drains from his heart in a pitiful groan
and the futile twist of a hand.
He curses the airborne blight that leaves
dead and dying bees.

This year's crop was hoped to return
a very profitable yield.
But there are risks and lives are lost
upon this battlefield.
And which of them would we think naive,
the keepers or the bees?

Autumn Bees

October was particularly warm this year.
We dared not say the "F" word for fear
that it might appear when we slept
but listened each day as the guaranteed high kept
approaching the twenty degree mark.
By seven o'clock it was dark
but late afternoons were ideal
for a bottle of wine and a barbecue meal
on the deck. Autumn leaves,
earth tone foliage, even the dying weeds
embellished the unseasonably warm
weather with seasonal colour and charm.

As we lounge in our comfortable chairs,
drowning our daily cares
in a full-bodied vintage,
fully content, fully engaged
in the prospect that this is the life,
Ah yes, this is the life!
Another bottle arrives,
is liberally poured then retired
out of the sun. Arriving too,
out of the sun, like a pair of intrusive
reconnaissance planes stealthily
scouting our mood, two bees
buzz the table from north to south,
one coming much too close to my mouth,
then go. Minutes later they or their friends
return from the north again,
this time with purpose. Sent
by the scouts, their rules of engagement
are simple; follow the fragrant trail
to its source, inhale
all available odours, dancing and darting around
'till the targeted substance is found.

Then attack! Bees with one purpose alone
are fearless, determined and bold.

Soon we are on the defensive.
Their numbers and aggressive
behaviour overwhelm us.
The yard is conceded. The battle lost.
Our retreat indoors
is inglorious.
Can these be the same bees
of Spring? Where is the 'please'
and 'thank-you' of April and May?
I know that Autumn bees have to make hay
while the sun shines, even in October.
Being bees they can't remember
six months back, but I swear
I can and my wine's out there!
Besides, Spring is far behind us and these
visitors won't leave. One can learn a lot from bees.

A Prayer On Suffering And Honey Bees

I do not suffer affliction with grace.
Pain and misery, wretch that I am,
inhabit my heart and set in its place
the fearful distresses of guilt and shame.
Easy to say give it over to God,
easy to say there is rest for my soul,
easy to say pass it off with a nod
and He'll do the rest, make me whole.
Easy to say for an angel or saint
shining triumphant in God's loving gaze.
Try gaining your feet when the light grows faint
and fainter and fainter each miserable day
as the darkness of Winter consumes from within.
I do not suffer affliction with grace;
self-pitying wretchedness cannot begin.
Empty and bitter, my courage a waste,
I beg for relief like a whimpering cur
awaiting another fall.

Mounted on a concrete hill
at St. Filbert du Pont Cherrault
in the village centre-ville,
Christ crucified. If you should go
notice that it's very plain,
a presentation unadorned,
stark as death, then look again
upon the crooked human form.
They'll tell you when you finally ask
what living memory can't restore
 that somewhere in the 'who knows?' past,
their village (one more to ignore)
gained a sudden curious fame.
This region of Les Tournesols
et fleures sauvages and gentle rain
crowned with plants and fertile soil,
abundance on a fertile plain,

is heaven for the honey bees
made cheerful by it all.

Be good to your servant and I shall endure
like the bees at St. Filbert whose hive is a cross.
Make Your ways known to me, show me that You
are my fortress, my safety, my refuge, my rock.
'Though my faults overpower me, set me apart,
teach me that suffering is good for my soul,
that Your words and your precepts are sweeter by far
than the sweetest honey that flows from the comb.
Like the bees at St. Filbert help me preserver
in You to seek shelter from troubles and men,
to look for the light through darkness and fear,
let Your spirit revive me, ignite me again.
Like the bees at St. Filbert each time dispossessed
by arrogant ignorant doers of good,
return and start over as your humble guests,
take me back to Your cross for a sliver of wood
as light as a shadow, more worthy than gold.
A weight for a pilgrim's soul.

Bird Watching

Red Cardinal on a leafless tree
in Spring, perched on an upper limb,
blackened eyes are watching me
whose searching eyes fixate on him.
I who keep this pleasant bower
ever since the world began,
find such pleasures in an hour
as to hearten any man.
Flashing feathers, rainbowed fish,
modest blossoms hung with bees,
a glass of wine, a whispered wish
from grandchild sitting on my knee.
A coat to keep the cold at bay,
a roof against the Wintery snow.
An ear to let me have my say
and miss my grumbling when I go.

Red Cardinal on a leafless tree
I bid you welcome to this yard.
We're not so different, you and me,
the world is ours but life is hard.
I hold dominion over you
who never held you in my hand,
nor lifted from the earth and flew,
nor understand my fellow man.
The firmament you daily ply
thickens like an evil doom.
The noxious effluence of my kind
rolls across the blaze of noon,
narrowing your sweep and mine
to cedar hedge, a chestnut dome,
a patch of grass, a scrap of time
entrusted for our common home.

Red Cardinal on a leafless tree,
a most emphatic bird you are!
Your plumage of humility
betrays you like a falling star.
Offspring of a royal line,
faithful champion to your spouse,
in human terms you well define
lord protector of your house.
But that gloomy image rises
when I brood upon our ills;
yours the freedom of the skies,
mine the burdens of free will.
Red Cardinal on a leafless tree,
could I ever be so true?
You bring your innocence to me.
What is it I can offer you?

Red Cardinal on a leafless tree
however this may sound absurd,
is it in your philosophy
to contemplate, being a bird?
Your enemies are on the prowl,
your green-eyed cousins ever near,
cause enough for me to frown,
cause enough for you to fear.
Your stoic posture in the face
of hostility is not
advisable. Go, quit this place.
Find a field of Bergamot
and spend the lazy Summer days
praying like a Capuchin.
Ah, me! My head is in a daze.
I dream. I dream a vapour dream.

Red Cardinal on a leafless tree
before you fly off to your nest
satisfy what puzzles me.
The blood-red mantle that you dress
marks you like an unearned sin.
You cannot hide from man or beast
in your busyness or still.
Will you ever be at peace
or know the ease of commonplace
without the weight of sacrifice?
And how do you endure the pace,
the hell-bound lunacy of life?
I look at you and heave a sign
and think I'm talking to myself
as seeing through an inward eye
my spirit on a wooden shelf.

At Lake Huron

A windy day at the beach.
Too windy. A gale, a tempest under
blue sun soaked skies.
We sat on the rocky shoulders
at the leeward side
of a garbled limb of rubble
that thrust itself out into the lake
like a stubborn tumour;
a spit of boulders separating
sand from stone.

Waves of brown wind
roared over our heads
as the beach was swept
from the flats into the calm
to be deposited at our feet.
A hundred years from now
the beach will be here.

By mid afternoon the few souls
who remained had dug their feet
into the sand, resisting the wind.
All the others had given up the battle
and gone home.
Blown away.

Later we were the sole survivors;
the thunderous wind, crashing breakers,
shifting beach, steadfast sun
and us.

Brown gale, brown boulders,
brown waters, brown limbs.
Rocky metaphors for troubled times.

Middle Island, New Brunswick

Salt and fresh water tides
embrace around a grassy
lump of turf
where the mighty Miramichi
ends its journey
to the sea.
A rich man with an eye
might covet this place
as a perfect retreat
from strife
where sweet and bitter meet.
Peace need not approach
nor joy, for all there is is sorrow:
"Bron, bron, mo bron,
sorrow, sorrow, my sorrow."

The passage itself was death
a century and a half ago
when Ireland's hungry nation
came in their coffin ships,
hungry hope in their hearts,
prayers on dry lips.
Like waters that mingle
together, despair
and promise became
the past and future forever
buried the same.
Hope need not approach,
nor rest, for all there is is sorrow:
"Bron, bron, mo bron,
sorrow, sorrow, my sorrow."

A visitor finds in his path
the usual memorial works,
a monumental stone, two flags,
a Celtic cross.
The rest of the island
is wind swept moss.
I stand with a heavy heart
unable to take
a step or speak.
The river surrounds
this grave where they sleep.
Dreams need not approach
nor linger, for all there is is sorrow:
"*Bron, bron, mo bron,*
sorrow, sorrow, my sorrow."

My crossing the ocean of tears
a hundred years on
was a bittersweet dream.
My ship was an empress
rolling on top of the waves
in jubilant dress.
In the immigrant's soul,
it shadowed but dimly
their sadness untold.
Grief and pain depart
and die, for all there is is sorrow:
"*Bron, bron, mo bron,*
sorrow, sorrow, my sorrow."

The Beach

He stood upon the desecrated beach,
a wounded man upon a wounded strand,
his eyes unblinking turned toward the East,
upon his back the setting sun's faint hand.
He thought the sand looked shallower than before,
yet who can gauge the depth of what is lost?
Now at the end of day he was footsore,
like a pilgrim slowed but never stopped.
                    Who misses a grain of sand?

His mind was running through the years behind
along a demarcation line of what
was in truth against what's fantasized
when all he knew of beaches was the hot
golden sand, hot Summer sun, the songs
of wind and cheerful waves, a young man's dream,
or maybe just a dreamlike moment gone
with all the intervening years between.
                    Who misses a grain of sand?

But here he was and this was not a lie.
The boardwalk had been lifted for a paved
highway convenient to cars and the like.
Cycloptic towers towered like great grey
guardians watching over everyone
for their own safety. Ice cream vendors sold
treats beside the rent-an-umbrella man.
And underfoot the sand was scant. Was cold.
                    Who misses a grain of sand?

Cape Split

The woods are awash and alive
with the mid-May glory of God!

Five petal flower whites
flash flood the forest floor
from the Bay to the Split,
like an uneven quilt
rolling over the swollen earth.

Fiddleheads gather in Mere Cat
clusters. Cautious. Expectant.
Their lifted green-eyed monocles
watch where I pass or stumble
over knobbled root knot
making my ramble a task.

There,
         where sunlight and shade
weave through the trees,
                              and there,
and there,
         regal purple trillium take
their proper place as matrons
in this fertile ward.

Now the silence is sweetened
by birdsong, joyfully so.
Now the trees are waking and stirring.
Beginning to show.

And I am the midwife of morning
making my rounds.

And God is the Father of everything.
Everything found.

In The Barn

In their small stall
two lambs newly born
a few days ago,
and the ewe
butting her head,
butting her head
against the unfavoured twin
as if she herself had known
spite and rejection,
is practising the lesson
now in a willful way,
not as a beast dubbed dumb.

In between blows
she nuzzles and kisses
the other, carefully mindful
of its injured leg.

Perhaps she safeguards the weaker,
punishes the fitter
in a bizarre reversal
of our expectations.
Perhaps she among the others
mothering their lambs
is the only militant feminist one,
determined to secure
her daughter's survival
over the male.
Perhaps she's obsessive-compulsive
disordered,
butting her head,
butting her head
for the pleasure that comes
when she stops.

We watch the unfortunate wretch
trembling in fear and disillusionment,
unaware of the tenderness
granted its sibling
the other side of the stall.
We want to explain to the mother
the moral incorrectness
of her behaviour,
carefully mindful of her
maternal prerogative.
To reform her in a loving way.
We want her to know
she is hurting herself as well,
butting her head,
butting her head.

Perhaps the shepherd is unaware
of the dangers herein,
needs to be informed, prepare
an intervention to mollify
this ideological unrest.

An Owl

If never before
I was mesmerized,
I am now.
Immobilized.
Root bound.
Fixed
intimidation.

The certainty
of its gaze,
calm,
confident,
accusing,
reduced mine
to nothingness.

Mottled brown-
feathered
beehive bird.
Fluent
buoyancy
held
in half light.

Irregular
black rimmed
dinner plate face.
Inverted triangle,
two black
olives,
one cashew.

Whose fixation
here anyway?
Your unblinking
inquisition
or my
nervous
inquisitiveness?

Go on stare.
Censure
my weakness.
Call my bluff.
While I covet
your complacent
composure.

Flight

December. An old reservoir pond
is feeling her age. Winter
has pressed his uninvited hand
against her breast. She shivers
at his touch and an icy grey flush
covers her skin in revulsion.
Her heart resists, resists.
Her extremities' warmth has gone.

For weeks she has been mother
to hundreds of ducks awaiting
the sign. They have clustered
around her fringes like children
fussing, fidgeting in pairs
and small groups asking questions.
The trail becomes a small stairs.
We soften our voices approaching.

Our presence disturbs them
into a sudden convoy quacking
through slurry and slush for open
water at the centre of things.
Behind us to the northwest
we notice what they already know;
the roiling, glowering test
of flight. The ducks and we must go.

Night Rain

Darkness. The heavy weight of silence.
Me under whitesheet, weighty
quilt, my bedroom a happy abyss.
Silent. Warm. Sleep's torpidity
numbing my mind like hemlock
as I sink and sink and sink.

A sudden shuddering cough
of wind on window pane, lunatic
and wild, jolts me alert against
my will. Then the rain as sudden
as gunshot and nearly as violent,
splattering again and again and again.

Wind on rain. Rain on wind. Storm
without, unrest within. Me unsettled
but certain of one thing; no harm
can come to me, nor be disquieted.
I am assured with every breath
a constant Sentinel to death.

Buttermilk

On any scale
churned cream becomes butter,
the left over liquid,
slightly bitter on the tongue,
its milk.

My father drank it
eyes closed, inverting
the bottle, squeezing
the last tart drops
from the glass,

smacking his lips,
sweeping them clean with his tongue.
Savouring the memory.
This is how I remember buttermilk;
my father's pint of white.

We must have been well off.
Only the less fortunate ate margarine.
We ate 'buther'
thickly spread like edible putty
on slabs of soda bread.

When Saturday mornings come around,
I rise early and construct
the week's supply,
reinventing the wholemeal
unavailable here.

Without precise measure,
it is never the same.
Some flour, brown and white,
bran, germ, oats,
soda, salt

and buttermilk
to churn it all
into a mortar coarse
mixture thick enough
to bind bricks.

Only the buttermilk
is the constant,
is the integrant
of past, present and future
imbibers and builders of bread.

Lie In

Nothing compelling bids
me move.
You are asleep beside me
breathing with enthusiasm,
soft putts erupt from
your lips, round
airy bubbles of spent air
out, life siphoned in
in measured wheeze.

Momentarily my mind is blank.
I tell myself in this instant
I know nothing, a pure, innocent
am. An infant Adam.

They arrive like vapour
through my porous skull;
wine-woven cobwebs spin
round my brain,
(memo to self, do not buy
that vintage again).
A snow event threatening the roof,
power outages likely,
God forbid, no more suicide
bombers please.

Daylight slips through slats
falling on the wall
like broken ladders.
Down the hall
heat pumps pump in warm air.
Outside cold silence
makes the bed feel more
comfortable.
I sigh deeply, lazily,
imagine the bed is floating.

I raise the covers
without purpose
admitting a cold draft,
igniting a shiver.
Foolish gesture.

Fragments of vanishing dreams;
a yellow cathedral,
airplanes,
crowds,
woman in a red dress.

New book, a gift,
more Seamus Heaney.
I spin a line,
"I am crushed by
the weight of your
weightless words."

Need a shower.

Morning prayers.

Out of muffins. Make more.

Would like another
hour of sleep but
that won't happen now.

All it takes
is one big solar flair,
poof, all communications
gone. Too dependant on
technology.
Some wise cracker
hacks the grid, smokes our power,
now what?
Bring back the horse.

Off home again this year,
THIS year.
May be my last visit there.
Getting too old.
Travel too dangerous.
What a sad world.

On the other
side of the bed
you shift your head,
ignorant of these
morning exercises
I perform,
nothing compelling me
to rise.

Lucidity

Someone who knows
said glass is a slow
moving liquid in the throes
of decay. Brittle
as first ice on a pond,
born of sequestered sand,
the glassblower's magic wand
breathing hot adrenalin
into inert bubble,
shaping, forming until
the sudden chill
inevitable crystallization.

And we, our crystallized
love time-sanctioned,
remember the lows and highs;
bedrock passions
like absolute molten
fire, icy silences when
we may never again
regain eye contact.
This slow moving dance,
this swaying, weaving advance
retreat, retreat advance,
like everything else, flows.

Spent Summer

I would pass the Summer sitting
on a painted tubular chair
on the deck we built one summer
when your mother wasn't here,
watching a bird in the birdbath
splashing about with her wings
splattering a million droplets
in the shimmering summer air.

I would pass the Summer listening
outside where my garden blooms
to the wings of butterflies flitting
from phlox to lily to rose,
wearing my old garden slippers,
my old tattered garden hat,
sitting beside the Hostas
pondering this and that.

I would pass the Summer spending
the days like a handful of coins,
found frivolous money burning
a hole in the pocket of time.
And when I run out of pennies
and the clouds have smothered the sun,
I will hibernate through the Winter
and await the arrival of Spring.

Family And Friends

Earth And Sky

My mother had said
that I'd looked
halfway to heaven
sleeping in the pram
she'd decorated in blue blankets,
blue crepe paper, blue ribbons
and a painted sign proclaiming,
'Rhapsody in Blue'
for the baby parade.
The first prize ribbon
pinned to the side
like a red slash
was decidedly out of place,
she'd recalled.

Once,
when I was able to sit,
she'd put me on the cool
grass in a park
and I'd started to cry,
then leaned forward
to deposit the last meal
I'd eaten between my legs.
After that, she'd said I was allergic
to grass.

I thought of these things while
watching sunlight penetrate
the Celtic Cross prism
hanging in the kitchen window
to fall across the counter in hues
of blue, red and green.
So long as I can remember,
I've always preferred the colour
green.

It seems to hold soothing
qualities, like memories of childhood,
or a yearning for something
unattainable.

I'm not distressed
to lie on a cool green
lawn anymore.
I remember looking
out the window of a jet
on its landing approach
in Ireland and thinking
that those beautiful green fields
look like a quilt
made by a giant hand.
I wanted to reach down
to touch them and feel their coolness.

My lawn is comforting
in Summer. It is
not the grass of childhood
but it is nearly as green.
Today it lies sleeping under
a layer of winter snow and ice,
but there is a blue sky
overhead spread across the world
like a mother's mantle.

The light through
the prism catches my eye
and I wonder how
that mother felt as she
looked upon her son
suspended halfway between
heaven and earth.

Boys And Men

I

We must have been eight
or nine before we learned
to walk. We couldn't wait
for anything to come
to us, Barry and me,
Summers and Saturdays gone
from dawn to dusk, full speed
forward friends forever.
And nothing to slow us down.
He was a natural runner.
Last house on the edge of town
where the Midlands canal
came to a sudden stop
at the crumbling terminal.
I struggled to keep up
on the long flat miles,
gangly limbs no match
for his fluid style.
At the waiting place he laughed.
And so did I.

We were experts of dung,
practising silent stealth
as we searched among
the cows the driest crusts,
prying with out boots
the lid from each jewel
box, gathering a loot
of pearly white mushrooms.
Confident thieves we were,
outwitting the horned beasts,
strutting like heroes home
to the evening feast.
There was nothing tentative
in our relationship.

The street where we lived
was simple arithmetic,
straight and friendly and known.
The canal and the pasturclands
were ours. We owned
it all. Our inheritance.
The present guaranteed.
And then the great subtract.
My father's shocking decree,
"We're going to Canada."

II

The day after Mothers' Day
I entered school,
my brogue a dead giveaway
in the yard and I must
be put in my place,
be jostled and pushed
into place because
it had to be done
and the big boys knew best.
Tom found me at the swings
and showed me a trick.
He was shaped like a violin.
A too tight leather belt
spread his bottom wide,
his upper svelte.
A vertical crop of black hair,
thick black spectacle rims
made him a friendly bear.

He took a wide stance on the seat.
"Now you get on board," he said,
"Between my feet."
Then he started to pump,
bending his knees on the 'to,'
his arms on the 'fro,' a pendulum

breezily swinging away,
confident Tom as the rod,
me the terrified weight.

Saturdays Tom came around
with his bike and lunch
and we flew out of town,
full speed forward,
gravel and dust in our wake,
me on the crossbar's
rattle and shake
finding a tentative trust.
Tom said the quarry belonged
to 'Al the bum'
and bringing me along
was a bit of a risk.
His camp was a canvas tent
badly built like a cow
reclined in a rocky wilderness,
ropes and cardigans, blackened pots
and a fire that never went out.
"Keeps the wolves at bay," he said.
That Summer the heat came to stay.
By August he was dead.

III

And we were moving again.
"To a Catholic school
with proper rules,"
my father explained.
City 'teens were different.
Fashion conscious,
networked, contemptuous,
subtle harassment
their weapon of choice.
Navy blue blazers,
grey pleated trousers

gave the school voice
but freedom wasn't for all.
One day after sweating
not once ever getting
a touch of the basketball,
when the cool guys
were trying to outgun
each other or run
up the score on the shy
un-athletic handpicked team,
a fellow was dressing
himself, carefully arranging
his clothes with extreme
almost fastidious care.
I was impressed.
How lovingly he took
the pants by the cuff
in one hand, the waist
in the right before sliding
a leg to the floor.
The same for the other.
A slick and admirable skill.

"They call me Mr. Clean.
It's a joke." He leaned
over and asked where
had I come from,
his manner casually
kind. He found my story
incomprehensible,
his questioning face
wanting more.
At the classroom door
he said, "Come over to my place.
We need to talk."
John's life was as neat
as his clothes, as complete
as a song, precise as a clock,

was "Going according to plan."
And he meant every word.

Years later I heard
he had joined the Canadian
Army. When he came back to town
I phoned. He laughed and feigned
an officer's superior air,
"I am a jewel in the Bwitish Cwown."
Then silence. To hear
a regret when nothing
is said is stretching
the moment too far.
But there it was,
an almost palpable,
perhaps even terrible
feeling. An inherited flaw
unspeakable to me?
A private taboo?
"Good talking to you,"
his feeble apology.

IV

It is said you can never
go home but I have.
Have wondered whatever
became of my town.
The canal is filled in.
The warehouse torn down.
Barry still lives in
the same house.
The priest mentioned
Alzheimer's disease.

Last Summer a famous
murder trial captured
everyone's interest.
Daily televised
updates kept viewers
like me mesmerized
for nearly a year.
A guilty verdict came down.
The prosecutor beamed.
It was Tom.

I drove to the city one night
and stopped to wait
for a change of lights
beside The National Hotel.
A figure I might have known
emerged, spread his feet
and watched a flood flow down
his pants, then stumble around
like a man with a wooden leg
crossing a ploughed field.

Saturday Mornings

So. Something Linda said
brought me to this scribbler
pen in flour-white hand.
Faint memory outflanked.
She said, before bringing
another buttered piece
of muffin to her mouth;
"Oh, how I love
these Saturday mornings!"

I find it uncanny,
even humourous, how
she always walks into
the kitchen as I lift
them to the countertop,
as if it was the first
time she tried my fare.
Faint memory outflanked.
A homecoming every week.

She Spends Her Days

She spends her days in busy-ness
forsaking time and place and brood,
for time and place breed bitterness
and so she marries to the wood,

shaping crossed and circled beams,
carving knowledge in the oak,
breathing life, infusing dreams,
passion's language every stroke.

Or weaving threads of flaming gold
around the green-soft bordered hem,
tells with images of old
the holy deeds of holy men.

Caught as in a rapture spell
her fingers while away the hours.
And thread and time are measured well,
for gold decays and light expires.

She knows but little discontent
and hums a half-remembered air,
when o'er the table she is bent
with floury hands and apron wear.

Her body and her mind delight
and find some triumph over age.
Another song is learnt tonight.
Another hundred lengths today.

And so they pass from rise to set
her waning years in busy-ness.
She has not known the loss, nor yet
embraced the suffering of rest.

Kitchen Photos

1

What memories do you have
of that day, glowing little girleen
with the milk pail?
Can you go back
through the black and white
and photo grey, tell me
your coveralls were pink
and the ribbons in your hair
a scarlet array?

There you are, in front
of the barn's west wall,
smiling into your father's
Brownie lens, stopped
with your empty pail.
"Don't move. Smile." Click.
"Gotcha. Go on now."
But you stood there a few seconds longer
smiling and dreaming. A few seconds longer.

I think you were smiling for me.
I think you were thinking,
"When I grow up I'm going to marry
a handsome man in a church
and I will be so happy.
And I will wear a white dress
instead of coveralls.
But I won't have a pail in my hand,
I'll have flowers instead

and a white veil on my head."
There is nothing more to record
except this; for the rest
of the world who knows
better than I, here's a black and white
snap on a farm in July
of an innocent long ago
fetcher of milk with a pail.
But I see where all others fail.

Always when I look at that picture
my heart is warmed by that little girl glow
and that secretive
Summer smile.
The one your father missed
by the barn's west wall
who thought you were happy at chores,
as you stood at the top of the aisle
smiling for me all the while.

2

There's a timorous uncertainty
in your posture that
had been learned long before
this holy day arrived.
A bearing of being
more familiar with solitude
than celebration when
you should have worn
the swagger of an heir to a crown.

The coat is too big
for your small frame,
unnew and distressed
by somebody bigger than you.
Even from here it appears

as a garment of resignation
unable to shape some
poise or possession, to confirm and hold
your place in the world.

Didn't anyone lick back
your hair or ask you to smile?
A turn to the light
and the deep dark umbra
drowning your eyes
soften away. Someone,
a priest, parent, a pal
standing at your side
could have encouraged some pride.

You would never conceive
such a desperate plan.
Affording no hope beyond
closing the day without fear
is there in your stance.
To let your mind run on other things
as boys do, like being a man
among men, vigorous, tall,
counters the being of small

You let us assume.
But wait! A smile, a very small
hint of a smile,
elusive at first, engages
like a beckoning unread book.
The plot within:
small town boy grows up,
runs away from home,
starts a new life on his own.

3

If anyone ever confined contentment
and peace of mind like two
willing prisoners in a tower
to nurture here day and night
it is you. Yours
is the place of unrestrained
harmonious well-being where mellowed
body and spirit concur.
One can almost hear your purr.

Still needing someone to lean on,
your husband arrived
like a cautious suitor,
intrudes himself into
the self-assured world
you profess. He has dwelt
too long in his faltering tower,
like the storm battered strongholds of old
with creaking stairways and cold.

After twenty-five years in this town
neighbours still call you "outsiders,"
"eccentric," "odd," "unconventional,"
a couple of antique curios
deserving revenge.
He for his "antisocial" mien,
you for your "litter" of kids;
an ungenerous generation
needing an explanation

to roll off their tongues.
Together you do make a mild contradict
as the photo attests.
You look the proverbial
pair of gloves,
one ineffective without the other
which must counter the first.
But the gossip will cease by-and-by
and the camera remain to apply

its exact indifference, finding you
deaf to the callous
din of the street,
glowing in feline contentment,
the love of your life
like a favourite blanket draped
easily over your arm.
Enduring disjointed agreeableness
these words have scarcely expressed.

Climbing Cedars

On St. Stephens' day Turlough said,
"If you want to find me
next Summer, look overhead."
In cedars where he can see
into second storey rooms
of this great house, feet
firmly stood on thick moon-
high boughs, he'll find a seat
and lord it over the rest
of us like a wren
when it dared to caress
the moon and claim again
that he was king.
I'll remind myself upon
all that's holy, calling
out to him as he bounces on
strong limbs beyond my reach,
that pride has no place beneath
a beckoning sky when a man must
look upward to find his fledgling son.

The Birdbath

In Summer the
pragmatic pedestal
of the birdbath
presents its
shallow water-filled
bowl for bathing birds.
In Winter
it summons snowflakes
from flight.

Couplet

The singular tragedy of my life;
I married a maths and sciences wife.

Dancing In The Kitchen

The friendly boards beneath the floor
are asked again to heave and swoon.
'Though dead a hundred years or more,
they dance when heard a merry tune.

Maple Villa

We built this house round its own bones,
its walls pulled down, tore up its floors,
reserved the ancient beams and stones,
the stained glass windows, crooked doors.

With paper rolls and tins of paint
we tried to find the former grace
that must have made it seem a saint
in flickering candlelight and lace.

A decade and four years have come
and gone. The house still moans and creaks
against a blast of winter wind,
against the rain the roof still leaks.
Racing feet and dirty hands
have redefined the stairs and halls.
We watch these architects at work
and wonder why we tried at all.

The Yard

For
five-year-old Turlough
there are exactly
twelve running strides
from the pump
to the climber,
a short journey of
four steps
up the ladder to the
five hand holds
he loves to traverse so long as
I am there below
supporting him.

It's hard to hear his laughter
over mine as I make my left hand
into a flat seat under his bottom
while holding his shirt with the other.
"You're tickling , Daddy,"
he calls.
"Don't let go!"
It's all I can do to avoid
his flailing legs until he reaches
the pole and slides down to the ground.

He sits on the grass contemplating
his next move. In front of him
the secret path to his neighbour's yard,
to his left a garden bench beneath
the chestnut tree,
the fish pond to his right,
and behind, sitting under the patio umbrella,
his smiling mother.

By our measures, his world here
is limited,
defined by trees,
challenges,
property lines.
He sees ordered security
and familiarity.
He is happy.

"Where's Ciarán, Mommy?"
"Out front playing in the cedar hedge"……
but Turlough has outrun her words
and is already there before she finishes the sentence.
"Stay away from the street,"
she adds automatically.
Only I hear the hint of fear in her voice.

"When I was that age," I say to Linda,
"We had the run of the street.
It was our backyard."
Every child in the neighbourhood played there
or in the yards.
In those days, the neighbours
looked out for us.
If a particular voice
went unheard, a mother would appear
in a doorway, a gesture
of visual supervision.

That was Harbour Street in Ireland.
It ended at the canal
and was as wide as the time it took
a five-year-old to leave his backyard
for the pub with his mother's coin
in his hand to buy
a loaf of bread for tea.
Where it began, only God
and "Long Tom" the Garda knew.

In those days, we knew
every face in every
doorway, and
every doorway
was ordered security.
We were happy.
Nowadays we look out for the neighbours.
Our world is defined by
property lines
and suspicion.
We are challenged
to bring order from chaos
in the neighbourhood.

Linda rises carrying her empty glass
around the house as she calls
the Irish names of her
Canadian sons.
She needs to see them.
"Over here, Mommy," they answer
as a car races by,
demolishing the speed limit.

Venus

Venus Boticelli stands on her
frozen concrete shell among the
frozen lily stalks
in my garden.
There beneath the sombre
morning sky, grey-veined by
leafless skeletons of trees,
she draws her hair around
her thighs,
and with her other hand
covers one breast.
Her slightly tilted head
and downcast eyes are lifeless,
concrete cold
and sad.
She seems to yearn for
something I can't give.
The summer sun, perhaps,
the warmth of life,
or more; the
longing gaze of men.

St. Francis

Among eternal blooms, eternal birds,
in sweet eternal peace, St. Francis lives
forever praising Him who ever is.
Forever in the presence of The Word.

And by my touch upon his stony brow,
I think to me a heavenly link he gives,
or momentary sweet communion brings
with that which we would call the Eternal Now.

But statues in November cannot tell
how days their light to darkness must concede,
how Winter feeds her own relentless need
to stalk with deadly cold each life-warm cell.

St. Francis' solid emptiness is cold.
Cold as the birds upon his sandled feet.
Cold as the eyes unblinking in this sleet
which drives across the darkening, dying world.

No comfort from the hooded robe or cross
he clutches to the place his heart lies still.
My hand withdrawn, I turn my back until
there is no holy union, only loss.

The man I am disclaims the act absurd.
Uncommon sense. A calculated whim.
The child in me is called to dance with him
among eternal blooms, eternal birds.

St. Anthony Of Padua

*"The greater you are, the more you should behave humbly,
and then you will find favour with the Lord."*

Eccles. 3:18

The Book spreads open mid seams
as a base for the saintly figure
holding the Holy Child.
My Book's bindings
stretched and bent
from years of uses,
reveals, on the pages
opened mid seams,
this Wisdom verse.

It would be easy to
dismiss as happy chance
and turn the pages
once or twice each way,
or seek another verse,
or close the Book without a glance.
It would be easy but
the saint would not go away.

I read his life
and came to understand
these nineteen words
fair implicate the man.

Rebekkah At The Well

What was he thinking when
he cast her in that nineteenth century
garb, a woman of God
leaning on the well like
a casual trollop?
The rain today has
left her weeping, a wet
veil of darkness
descending to her feet until her tears
have soaked into the soil.
I ask myself aloud;
"Why does she weep?"
Is it because she
must forever stand
and suffer silent loss
of rain-dyed pride?
Did he not know that
by his careless hand
he gave her sin, and thus
she weeps inside?
Or does she grieve for us
who, like her form,
have turned ourselves
from sacred to profane?

The Climber

Like a tall disembodied
spider, the climber
sticks its four cold
tubular steel legs
into the frozen ground.

From one of its two
protruding arms a
piece of yellow rope
sways helplessly.

The snow covered
blue seat of a swing
hangs below the other.
Empty.

When this winter's over
the cries and laughter
of my children will
awaken the climber
like a butterfly
from its shell.

The Pump

It couldn't be done barehanded
but if I put a rope around
its throat it might be
ripped out easily enough.
It had to go
because it was there,
in the way,
even 'though the path
ran past it.
It had no function.
Without an arm it was
useless,
a limbless rusting
twist of iron
thrusting through rotting
floorboards
which covered
a barren shallow hole.

I didn't want to do the act,
just thought it must
be done. Then I relented.
I remembered a working roadside
pump on the way to school.
It was forbidden to children,
I knew that much.
Only for grownups with
empty battered buckets,
of a leaning post for banter,
or for forming a bowl
with dirty work-worn hands
to quench a horse or donkey.

One day it was alone
like me.
The stretch of road
was empty there and back,
the only witness
a cloud-blinded sun.
I didn't want to do the act,
just thought it must
be done. With fury
and guilt
I pumped and
pumped and
pumped,
forcing in front
of the flood
a sharp shuddering
belch of air then
the surprising splurge
of water jack-
hammering the earth,
sending brown splatter
evidence of sin
over pants,
legs, socks
and shoes.

The pump
is still there,
blocking my way to the yard.
It's painted black now,
and is useless as before.
I'd have pulled it out long ago,
only I really don't want
to uproot it.

From The Pew

In nineteen forty-eight or forty-nine
she squeezed my fragile shoulders with a vow
I still can hear her whisper through a smile,
"Stay here, I'll be back in a bit," and how
she disappeared into the shuffling crowd.

And I would make some comfort
if I twined
my bony little fingers
in a weave,
and searched with bony knees
the rough to find
the little wooden valley
of a crease.
Then close my eyes and hide
inside a sigh.

Afraid to lift my head,
I would pretend
my elbow was a turnstile
and if I
just moved it barely past
the bench's end,
I'd count each coat or sleeve
that shuffled by
until the last one
left me all alone.

A child can only talk of time as 'long.'
A long time might be Daddy coming home,
or counting down the sleeps 'till Christmas morn,
or being afraid of what he doesn't know
and holding fast his breath 'till she returns.

My mother never tells me
why she arose
with all the others
plodding like a heard
of cattle needing milking.
I suppose
I'm just too little
or I don't deserve
to get whatever treasure's
being shared.

But when I feel her
nudging at my side,
I smile a secret smile
and sideways glance
in time to see her shield her face
and cry
into her Sunday gloves.
I take a chance
and try to tell her something
but I can't.

Slinking back into
my little room
where solitude and silence
let me be
removed a little distance
from her gloom,
I want to understand
why is it she
is crying
and forgotten about me.

And then I grit my teeth
and squeeze my eyes
and make my little hands
into a fist.
When I am big, I vow,
who made her cry
I'll get into that line
with all the rest
and punch him on the nose,
my very best.

My mother died in nineteen ninety -four,
my family joined me at her funeral Mass.
The youngest lad, a terror at just four,
had shed his tears for Nanna and had asked
familiar questions any child might ask.

At the appointed time I took his hand
and found our place among the shuffling line.
I still remember how this little man
smiled and whispered, "Daddy is it time
to get my blessing?" And I almost cried.

Granddaughter

The immediate question arises;
did Saoirse (suddenly my eyes
look at that word and I wonder
did I or did I not spell her
name correctly?)

No hurrahs for recent memory.

Did Saoirse dictate her thoughts
to you, God's new daughter
on loan to you her father,
Angela her mother,
engaging your eyes,
undistracted by the surprise
of hands and feet;
did Saoirse, her still incomplete
language skills, demand of her
limbs other signs for you to decipher
into poetry?

Or is her just
being your creative catalyst?

Lucy. (b. 1918, d. 1994)

This was my mother.
A free and bog-born woman of Ireland
with fierce blue eyes, grinding jaws
and penetrating will dispensed
by equally commanding tongue;
whose small hospital room
had become her monastic cell,
far from home
for more than a decade.
A woman whose wit
bent my body with laughter
over stories of "Sideways,"
(because she walked that way)
and "Kit the Man,"
(because she looked like one),
both bog-born and free.
A woman whose own body
arthritically tortured and
twisted, bent itself
into a knot over four decades,
and she denying it
the pleasure of even
a whimper.

This was my mother.
A body strapped into a wheelchair
beside the Poteen at Christmas,
lips wet and smiling,
her fork stuck in the plum pudding
and boneless hands pressed against
each side of her glass which
jigged and reeled to the music
stirring long ago memories
savoured behind closed eyes.
Not a care in the world.
Not a care in the world.

This was my mother
whose arms formed a cross
where an elbow should be,
whose dry transparent
ulcerated limbs called legs
pulled under an arching back
in her crucifix hospital bed
succumbing to spasms,
pain, seizures
and more pain, and she
defiant, determined,
calling out with all
her spirit and will,
"Hail Mary, full of grace
the Lord is with thee….."

This was my mother,
free once more beneath
Mary's blue mantle,
surrounded, surrounded by angels!
Her body no longer a cause.
She is silent and still
to my presence, but
her eyes are softened
and focused. Her eyes
are talking and lively
and talking.
But not to me.
Her cell is a holy place.
I am standing on holy ground.
And Mary at last comes
to take her home.
And I pray,
and I silently say,
"This is my mother.
I think you know each other."

The Feis

The early morning drive
to 'The Falls'
is a dirty one.
Around us grey skies meet
grey horizons while
dirty grey slush
from last night's snowfall
splashes on passing cars.

Two bodies slouch
in the van's back seats
still under the covers of heavy eyelids.
                              The slap-
slap-slapping
                    of the wipers
has reached a pair of feet
which joins in the rhythm,
rehearsing themselves, if not their owner
for the test.

We are travelling the two hour
journey to the *Feis*.
There, my daughters
will undergo a metamorphosis;
there,
wearing faded jeans,
oversize long sleeve sweat tops and
helmets of pink plastic curlers,
they will enter a crowded change room,
emerging a few minutes later
almost unrecognizable.
They will have become
dancers.
Resplendent in splashing costumery,
ancient gold, green, while symbols
on brilliant blue velvet.

Rich crimson capes bearing
embossed Tara brooches in saffron,
embroidered purple knot work,
a Celtic cross,
and springing curls, real or near-real,
they preen themselves in pairs,
meticulously inspecting each other
for a disobedient strand of hair,
too much blush here, not enough there,
straight, even, bubble sox,
and on it goes.

The hotel ballroom
quickly fills with daughters
and anticipation.
I can feel the anxiety in the air,
hear last minute encouragements from mothers,
worried voices from ambitious teachers,
everything in double time,
                    speech,
      step,
            breathing,
                touching,
                    greeting.
All must be done
before the announcement calls them to
their imagined highest destiny.
Then it comes,
always garbled,
always unintelligible,
always clearly understood;
      "All dancers for competition one-oh-one,
      please report to stage three immediately."
A quick kiss and
away we go.

My friend has joined me at the coffee table.
He forces a smile across an unshaven face.
"I should be home in my warm bed.
It's just gone eight o'clock."

This is a ritual.
We tour the circuit
a dozen times each year,
each stop starting earlier than the last,
it seems.

The next move is to the stage
where, with luck, we find a chair
to which we'll become attached
for the next nine hours.

My middle daughter Roisín
is wearing number 130.
She is standing at the back
of the stage
waiting her turn,
a very relaxed and patient
approach to dancing
and life.
This is a soft shoe reel.
The accordion player has already
played the tune
ten times over
but it still sounds fresh and lively.
By the end of the day,
his left arm will be bandaged,
the beat have abandoned his foot
and his lunch dried on the plate
beside his chair.

Roisín steps forward,
points her toes,
picks up the tempo,
and,
		hop, cut-jump, hop cut-jump,
		twist kick but-ter-fly, twist kick dip.
Now the left foot.
		one-two-three, one-two-three,
		turn-two-three and,
DOWN
		SHE
					GOES!!
She has landed ingloriously
mid-stage,
smiling
while the judge regains his composure
to jot a brief note on the scoresheet.
Roisín knows.

She is still for a moment,
enjoying the situation.
Then, she rises,
picks up the music,
		on time, in step,
		two-two-three,
		two-two-three,
		Stop!
A crisp bow to the table,
and off the stage.
Her friends surround her.
		"That's how it goes," I whisper to my friend.
		But she'll be ready for her hornpipe."

The day takes other tolls:
a teen places second
and storms from the stage
unsatisfied.
Another is backed to the wall
by a mother scolding
and waving a finger in her tear-filled face.
The hastily fastened hairpiece
on a fierce competitor
quits its place before the music stops.
She executes a beautiful
scissors jump
on top of it,
and like Roisín, it remains still.

The hours wear on,
music drones,
performers retire
and leave in groups
designated by age.

This is the pattern of
the *Feis,*
the rhythm of life.
Some call it
"The same old same old,"
and so it becomes.
Some
"Fix their eyes
and go for the prize."
And win!

What sets them apart?
I think one dancer is
better shaped,
more compact than the rest,
gravity centred to suit the skill.
There is greater determination

in that one.
This one has practised
until her calves
are steely hard,
her steps
precisely
crisp.
   "Maybe true," my friend says.
   "It depends on what the judges
   are looking for."

At two o'clock
Roisín and I are watching
the main stage
where Niamh will dance.
The judges have come from
Ireland, England and America
looking for something,
for world championship style,
looking for…

Niamh remembers
last month's advice on
a single sheet of paper.
   'MORE ATTACK.'
As always she is composed.
As never before
her eyes are focused.
Her number is called,
the music begins,
a piece for hard shoe called
The Drunken Gauger.
   Stamp-up-kick, down and out,
   treble-up and treble-back.
   One-two-three, one-two-three,
   click heels and down-two-three.
Her posture is perfect,
her arms are in lock.

She drives through the cadence,
I pull out of shock.
The first minute and a half
is top form!
She dances with vigour!
She dances with joy!
She is ON!

The next ninety seconds
last forever.
As energy depletes,
shoulders sag,
weary legs grow lazy
and reluctant feet are forced
to the finish.
Finally, it is over.

She must dance twice more
today
then wait for results
another two hours.
This is the pattern of
the *Feis,*
and so,
we wait.

      "Well?" I ask.
      "I think I'm tenth or twelfth,
      I don't think I placed,"
      she says flatly.
Daylight is fading outside,
the ballroom is quiet.
Caretakers begin sweeping
empty areas.
Only the arrogant and
the dreamers remain.

At last the convener steps forward
to announce,
>"There are eight awards to be given,
>the top six qualifying for the world
>championships.
>In eight place competitor number
>seventeen…"

I glance at Niamh's card with a large
three on it.
She shifts in her chair.

>"In seventh place competitor number
>eleven…"

She sighs and removes her hair band.
It's time for us
to go home.
>"In sixth place, competitor number
>three…"

My heart stops.
>Niamh's EXPLODES!

We are both in tears.

She rushes forward
to the stage where
everything happens in
double time,
applause,
>a hug,
a blur,
>a lifelong memory.

When she returns,
clutching her award,
Roisín greets her with
warm admiration.

> "You're going to Ireland, Niamh,
> you're going to the World's."

Our drive home
through a dark dirty night
is uneventful,
but the back seats
are alive!
Voices rise and fall,
laughter brightens the space
enclosed by the van,
and for two weary
dancers,
the rhythm of life
is toe-tapping
through
tireless
feet.

Nuala

With loving hands I smooth your hair
to win a smile, my wounded Nuala Ann.
Your waking hours are spent, I fear
in conflict. All my smoothings only fan
the spark of anger through your veins.
Then tears arise and voices seldom heard
are edged and sharpened, cruelly thrust,
'till I must surely die with every word
I speak, or tell my heart its pain
will fade into tomorrow when once more
we try out mettle, test our verve.
O loving child! O waking womanhood!
Your will is in your making. In your blood.

Legacy

When I was thirty years and two
I was king of the world.
I had it all.
A wife, a home and children (two),
teaching career secure as gold,
friends and admirers coming to call,
all of us glowing and in our prime,
rarified air, roses and wine,
when I was thirty years and two.

And now that I am sixty-four,
and you have reached
the age of kings,
and you are standing at my door,
a moving van your royal seat
and all my world diminishing.
Regarding your imperial mien,
I slink aside as you sweep in,
a courtier at sixty-four.

Tiarnan

As if the language
between sunrise and sunset
was woefully inadequate,
you choose instead to express
your exuberance in throaty
gurgling, clapping hands,
unimagined delight discovered
in the littleness of his being.

How could you expect
to contain yourself or him?
Only six months ago
he was battering knowledgeless limbs
against the cage of your ribs,
like a faultless inmate
testing for faults,
exploring the swell.

Little moon-faced man
from far away,
struggling against gravity
sitting hands-free at her feet.
Already you begin
to pull away,
oblivious to the safety
of her hands behind your back.

Coming Home

When to his amazement he say
that the weekend was light, Ciarán
came home. Third year scholar, his eyes
were flashing with childlike delight
as he hugged his mother, but broke
from her dreamt-of embrace and took

a run at his brother who crushed
him breathless. Man-like. Robust.
My turn would come later on
when the wine had loosened our tongues
and our bellies (after the feast
of chicken and chocolate and cheese)

uncomfortable full, disengaged
from the ruins, to loll and drape
over sofa and soft comfy chairs.
Two lazy boys splayed like a pair
of old pals. At ease. Laid back.
Perfectly poised for attack.

Ciarán was as cool as a jazz
singer. Serene and controlled,
even seductive. He posed
a silent prelude then spoke
this pre-emptive volley of words;
        "Batter my heart, three-personed God
        ...Nor even chaste, except you ravish me,"

shattering the understood rules
of engagement. Invoking the muses
of Celtic lore always came first
like a statute of sacred trust.
The others might enter the fray
to back up the cause of the day
but could never lead. This affront

was a treacherous blow clearly meant
to disable me from the start.
But his infamous act fell short.
Regrouping on opened ground
I turned the encounter around

with grace and finesse. I exposed
his unguarded passionate soul;
        "And some time take the time to drive out west
          …and catch the heart off guard and blow it open."
He offered a disarming smile.
By now we had had too much wine

but were off on a friendlier game
where the only thing left to gain
was the wonder of words and wit.
Heaney and Yeats out of habit
were read as were Hopkins and Donne.
Then the writings of father and son

slipped into the medley. Ciarán
in true to form graciousness, yawned
a kindly reminder of place.
And we stopped. And gave thanks. And embraced.

House For Sale

She said she knows
it's time to go,
and yet she would not shift.

This house is
full of echoes now,
the rooms are twice
as big somehow.
The mornings come
on slippered feet
these days but
they are bittersweet.

The bathroom door
is opened wide,
the shower curtain
pulled aside.
The breakfast din
at start of day
is long ago
and far away.

No one is rushing
for the bus
for now there's
only two of us.
The dredges from
the pot of tea
are old and cold
by half past three.

There's apple pie
from yesterday
and oatmeal cookies
on the tray.
Laundered socks
come back in twos,
there's no mistaking
whose is whose.
The hallway's wooden
boards are still,
the floors are clean
of spots and spills.
And later, five or
ten past four,
no one is bursting
through the door

with tales of how
the school day went,
the teachers' faults,
the time ill-spent,
the latest crush,
the team's defeat,
and "Is there
anything to eat?"

Around the supper
table there's
no clamouring for
favourite chairs.
No little voice
and hands held where
we all joined in
the blessing prayer.

Tidy straightened
empty beds
lie undisturbed
by sleepyheads.
But more than that,
what most is missed
is, "Good night, Mommy"
and goodnight kiss.

This house is full
of echoes now.
The rooms are twice
as big somehow.
She says she knows
it's time to go.
And yet she will not shift.

Moving Day

I woke this morning with the light
'twas in the month of May,
I heard the sound of chirping birds
announce the break of day.
The parent was returning with
the first meal of the day,
and as she flew back to her nest
she called as if to say;
   here I come,
   here I come,
   I wasn't far away.
   Here I come,
   here I come.
   I'm never far away.

My memory was carried back
some fifty years or more,
a little boy is standing at
an empty cottage door.
He doesn't want to leave behind
the only life he knows,
and when his mother takes his hand
it's time for them to go;
   Robert come,
   Robert come,
   you know we cannot stay.
   Robert come,
   Robert come.
   We have to sail away.

The years rolled on and soon my
mother wasn't at my side,
but I had found a happy home
to share with my new bride.
Our family began to grow
and we were filled with pride

to see our children laugh at play
and hear their gentle chide;
> Daddy come,
> Daddy come,
> Daddy come and play.
> Daddy come,
> Daddy come,
> Before we fly away.

And now my heart is heavy
for the thing that I must do.
To help my daughter pack her things
and start a life anew.
They're off to Nova Scotia
and my eyes are filled with dew
as I wave goodbye to my grandchild
and hear her calling too;
> Grandpa come,
> Grandpa come,
> Grandpa come and play.
> Grandpa come,
> Grandpa come.
> We're not so far away.

Admiring A New Car In The Mall

Bald. Pudgy.
Hands planted in pockets
like handles around
a round beer belly,
unable to stand erect,
he slouches forward
precariously,
peering into the
driver's side window,
his expressionless
stubbled face
staring back
without admiration.
His coat sleeves
reflect ambient light
like black ice on asphalt.
Winter has wearied
his runners,
faded his trousers,
scattered his sure-fire schemes.
His breathing is
ponderous.
Shifting his focus
between image
and icon,
he wastes another minute
and wonders how the hell
he got to be this way.

Grandchildren

What is it that delights me most?
My books dropped to the floor,
this happy host of fairy folk
come dancing through the door,
tumbling, bumbling limbs a-fly
like prancing lambs in May.
They laugh and call for very joy
and lift my dreamy day.
I marvel at their play and how
they sport in everything.
For I am in my Winter now
and they are in their Spring.

This one's dolly has a bruise
that only we can see,
and when I call out "Go!" he'll prove
there's no one fast as he.
It seems we've had a falling out,
I can't remember when,
but there's that stony silent pout
and I'm at fault again.
I beg in vain to please allow
for weary lungs and limbs,
for I am in my Winter now
and they are in their Spring.

The lads have found a weathered ball
and raising battle cries,
tug my body down the hall
oblivious to its sighs.
Close behind three curly heads
are calling, "That's not fair!
There's twenty stories to be read
and brothers have to share!"
Caught in these familiar sounds
old memories rise and ring,
for I am in my Winter now
and that was in my Spring.

Too soon, too soon they've gone away
on little magic feet.
Whispering spells in other ears,
the circle is complete.
I bend to fetch their scattered toys
and find an elfin smile
hidden behind these heavy eyes,
but only for a while.
This house is filled with ghostly forms
of dim-lit childish things.
I hear the howl of Winter storms,
they the songs of Spring.

Moonstruck

In these latitudes winter's black
velvet nights arrive mid-November
cold-aged and deep as space,
awaiting the first snowfall's inevitable
glowing white bright face.

One night after supper you looked
through lacy curtains in sudden
astonishment. A full moon took
possession of the sky, cool
and confident as a seasoned con-man.

"Moon! Moon!" You announced,
pointing excitedly, pyjamed and ready
for bed. "Moon! Moon!" Grabbing a wrap,
I ambushed you before your Mommy
could object and stepped outside

into the undernourished air,
your sudden wide-awake littleness
fighting my embrace. But where
the folds parted, you looked skyward
and swallowed the moon with your eyes.

As we stood against the rail,
my limbs numbing, you learning
the latitudes of night and moonlight,
I wondered what trails you were blazing
across the wonder-filled sky.

Since then you have gone every night
to the window after dark,
every night for thirty nights
pointing to the same place.
"Moon? Moon?" You search and ask.

We have faithfully stepped
into the velvet cloak of darkness,
swept the moonless night sky east
to west. Disappointed. Unimpressed.
Longing for moonlight and snow.

How can you, your simplest
expectations nightly slipping away,
clouding your eyes, bruising your heart
begin to understand your need for light?
Or know the fixed star on which we wait?

Then last night that conjurer
came back. "Mooooon!" You called,
and tugged me to the door.
When you were tangled up in blanket and arms
you might have tried to fly!

Little boy that you are,
you cannot see the moon
for what it is. Thief. Hustler.
Cold-fired light. A two-faced
dispassionate lunatic, calling you

to its embrace where nothing can live.
Cling to your blanket a moment.
Struggle against what is safe.
Land with your feet on the ground
as you search for the fixed star.

A Fence In The Way

When we stopped to look
at the chickens and hens
and the lop-eared rabbits
and talk to them,
I felt the warmth
of the sun depart
and a cloud's dark shadow
encroach my heart.
And I said, "Little grandchild
we better run
the half-mile back
to get us home
before we are drowned
by a sudden rain."

But you were pulling
against the straps
that couldn't secure you
or hold you back,
and were there not
a fence in the way,
you, bunnies and 'bok-boks'
would soon be at play.
And scattering fowl
as if shot from a gun,
would terrorize rabbits
and add to the fun
of stumble and tumble
and unrestrained glee.

But I being shackled
by grownup wit,
getting wet in the rain,
wanting none of it,
wisely bringing
the stroller about
hustled the two of us
back to the house.

Later that evening
in my feathered bed,
I offered my prayers
for 'bok-boks' instead,
and bunnies and children
and rainy days.
And I wish had yielded,
and wish I had stayed.

Faydra

Let us not praise the deeds of important men;
give them their quarter hour of fame
or eternity of infamy,
then never speak of them again.
Let the world say, "He brought a crowd to their feet,"
or "Multiplied the profits sevenfold," or
"Restored great honour to a broken throne."
But some tomorrow when we chance to meet
we shall not talk of them.

Instead, you and I will speak of little ways
that pass unnoticed like a faltering flame
flickering thrice before finally going out,
not having known a glorious blaze.
We will embrace to hide our momentary grief
and find some comfort there
searching for the proper words
to soften awkward heaviness and grief,
but we shall not find them.

I will ask you to recall for me
how she welcomed every precious day
pushing pain aside for little joys
which you and I can never hope to see.
In this way we will come to know, I think,
the triumph of one small determined girl,
bullied by blindness,
crippled by cancer, prodded and poked to the brink,
and we shall be saddened.

Then, forsaking sorrow, you will smile
and say, "She didn't like the feel of grass
under her feet or walking up hills.
She would stare at her hand for the longest while
then shake it and laugh."
I will remember her curly brown hair
bouncing like bubbles when she'd
look at my face close up and laugh.
And we will be laughing.

The deeds of important men? What are these
compared to the towering heart
that dwelt in the breast of such a child?
Oh, how God must have been pleased
to welcome his little darling home
like a conquering hero returned
the evening she took her leave
from this valley of tears.
And you and I will agree.

The Walking Man

The walking man comes walking
by no more.
Sad to say I haven't seen him
pass my door
this year, nor is it likely he'll
come trudging through
this deep December snow and cold.
Was it you
who said he must have died?
After the fact
I find myself thinking that by
the simple act
of appearing on our street
each mid afternoon,
he was like a knot tying
sun and moon
together, equidistant between my rising
from and falling
into sleep. His appearance,
witnessed or taken
for granted, was my personal equinox.
I needed him
as a ship needs an anchor to
hold it still.

Darwin is enjoying a remarkable
resurgence these days
among scientists decoding the stuff
known a DNA,
that spiral staircase message board
in every living
thing. An endless evolutionary stretch
of elastic string
drawing primitive pre-man to man.
What Darwin could
never have known in his primitive art

bad and good
science, taut as a Gordian knot,
is coming undone.
Becoming yesterday's dubious news
lacking in fashion
and style, falling to earth
in a heap.
Layer by layer, minute by minute,
murky and deep
secrets once known only to God, now
and for all
intimate; the walking man must first have
learned to crawl.

The photograph you treasured most
is perfectly clear.
Smiling eyes and blue, complexions
light and fair,
body shapes more than less the same,
tie our clan
together genetically. Invisible
beyond the camera
lens, furtive features inhabit
the soul's domain:
the sorrow of an aging mother's heart,
a will ordained
towards a higher end. A dark reserve.
And now I
will arise and walk the snowy streets
and pass by
someone's door. And I will meet
another walking man
and listen to his wisdom
while I can.
And all that he will say is,
"Keep the zeal!"
And all that I will hear is,
"Herod will fall!"

O'Hagan

He asks me again and again
the questions that tug at my soul without mercy.
I shuffle along beside him, head bent
like a reluctant schoolboy
trying to find the right words
to explain a promise unfulfilled.
There is spring-loaded desperation
in his voice. A tangible tension
can be seen in the line
of his jaw-clamped face.
"You remember that marker
we pinned to the trees
for the orienteering course?
The one that read, 'Keeping going,
you're on the right course.'
That's all I want."
He spat out the last words like they were venom.
By now the light sensors
on the street lamps
had started to flicker
their silent alarms
to signal the approaching gloom.
The sky is black, the asphalt black,
the houses merely dim unfamiliar shapes.
It was that moment of doubt
when urban confidence whimpers a little
before the darkness is finally dismissed.

I nod to his question an affirmation
that at once binds our friendship
and confirms my attention
'though the gesture is futile and blind.
I assume his anxiety.
I am scarred by his self-inflicted wound
but I fail to steal his pain.
That's all he wants, he says,
That's all.
Just a sign that says
keep going, you're on the right path.
And on we walk in the dark street
and in the tragic irony
that eludes us like the flickering
uncertain light.
It is the question that poses the answer.
It is the prod at the soul
that pushes us forward, on course, on time.
But my tongue is silent and still
as the stars.
There is no vocabulary taught
to unravel this knot.
Voices rise up from an open door
and we wave in response
to the friendly curfew.
Our steps are quickened as if
to outpace this heavy encounter
with living and the
unremitting subtlety of God.

The Girl With The Three-Legged Dog

She's fourteen years old
living out her last days,
a misshapen marriage of rattle and fur
hauling a limb of reluctance behind
like a curse.

Her muzzle is grey
and her breathing betrays
the effort it takes her to hobble along,
rising and falling without any sort
of a plan.

I see her each day
coming up the side street
avoiding the hustle and bustle of man,
forsaking the pavement for friendlier foot—
hold of grass.

She stops for a scratch
and a few soothing words,
collapses her frame on the cool of the lawn
extracting a measure of joy from the toil
of her day.

She's a mangy old mutt
with a dubious past,
tethered by time's too dispassionate grip,
unworthy of life were it not for the light
in her eyes.

The girl with the three-
legged dog is not old.
She's fair and she's slender and carries the grace
of a woman portraying the prime of her life
to the world.
Her garments are current
and chosen with care
to tastefully flow with the languorous pace
she maintains for the dog and the eyes of the men
she might meet.

An air of detachment
precise and controlled,
heightens the mystery engaging the mind
as she stops or is stopped by the dog where I sit
near my door.

Some meaningless words
are politely exchanged.
She talks of her love for the dog who responds
by licking her hand and an efforted thump
of her tail.

The girl with the three-
legged dog tugs the leash,
removes her sunglasses and passively states
that her marriage has failed, and a cloud passes
over her eyes.

The Death Of Conceit

Holds his big left hand
before his face
to cover from startled eyes
his whole enormous
tongue lolling
out of his mouth
like a lifeless thing.

His eyes betray
frustration as he
shoves the flesh
back into its cave,
slamming his teeth shut
to keep it in while
noisily slurping
coffee from his cup.

Some pristine patrons
recoil and leave
their table when his
quick right hand
wipes away the drool
as the tongue falls out again
faster than his left hand
can conceal it.

Others stare in silence,
their own mouth
agape;
their lack of sensitivity
a greater infirmity
than his.

I turn away to give
him back his stolen dignity,
and to avert my eyes
from his,
fearful that he'll penetrate
my pitiful embarrassment
and try to comfort
me.

Relic

A curt black and white notice
pinned to the post office wall
told me Wilf was dead.

That was Tuesday.
Next day it was gone, buried
with the rest of the trash.

It wasn't until the weekend
that his eulogy was given
by dozens of black-coated

mourners, chattering in inexplicable
confusion under the dying maple,
waiting in vain for his

morning arrival to feed them.
Wilf bought a pair of black
army boots at our garage sale

one Spring, 'though I never
saw him hiking or marching anywhere.
He was a bike rider

from another era. It was
his trick to flash his right
boot at me, up and down

like a yo-yo while his left
foot pistoned awkwardly
up and down, up and down,

pulling the bike from side
to side, off-balance
as he trundled along to stop

inevitably beside the tree,
spray a handful of peanuts
around and wait.

He was a railway relic;
a living poster for a coal man
in his crumpled black and white cap,

baggy colourless coveralls,
red rag hanging from his rump
and a scruffy salt-and-pepper beard

encroaching on water eyes and nose.
An eccentric loner.
A side-glanced and whispered

n'er-do-well in this village
of arts. Wild cats and tame
knew his corner cottage,

coming and going
for scraps and affection,
giving affection in return

before disappearing into
the overgrown jungle of broken
asphalt and ties

that once was the end of the line.
He endured man and beast
unruffled and honest as youth.

"I have no regrets," he told me
the last time we talked
across his bicycle.

I think he knew
his time was up and wanted
someone in this offending

place to miss him.
He never spoke of family
or a woman in his life

but was a natural for
harmless gossip.
I loved his unpredictability,

breezily granting an entire morning
one day, then turning a cold shoulder
the rest of the week.

He could be as easy and hard
as the weather, but never mean.
I couldn't guess his age

and the notice didn't say.
His cottage was razed a few
days along with the rest

of the rail lands. There's a pin-neat
park there now, straight across
from my front door.

Twelve Months

January

Suddenly air is roaring
from holes in the floor
for the third time this hour.
Roaring like an imprisoned
tornado, forcing
a torrent of furnace-forged
heat persistent and loud
as an ill-tempered wind.

Closed doors help me
believe I'm cutting down drafts,
keeping the rooms
warm where most
of Winter's deep freeze
days are passed.
January is the tomb
of the year and I am cold

as a corpse.
Impoverished of sunlight
by day, buried in blankets each
night, I curse the interminable snow
which shows no remorse.
Summer is nowhere in sight.
Its frontiers are well out of reach
and the borders are closed.

February

'Though you grumble and grunt
in your malcontent ways
like a child growing out of his shoes
before they conform,
or kick up your heels
like a filly at play
who leaps like a startled gazelle
at every unknown.
'Though your shiftless improvident
ill-defined days
moored at the midriff of Winter
meander along,
or you torment the prospect
of Spring on a vagabond
breeze with false promises sworn
in a songburst of sun.
'Though you yearn and you sigh
in your transient grave
for someone to love you
before you move on,
I rejoice and am saddened
in your incompleteness,
your bittersweet briefness of presence.
And then you are gone.

March

Spring gave me her
calling card today
and then she fled away.
Away to the South
She sped
calling back as She left,
"Turn down the bed,
throw open the shutters,
unbutton your coat.
Take a deep breath of me
for I shall return.
I shall return turning
the ice-grey snow
to rivers run wild.
Like an unrestrained
jubilant child,
I shall dance down your street
on hyacinth-daffodil feet
budding the hedgerows
and trees.
I'll hide-and-go-seek
with the breeze
playing tag in the pullovers
pinned to the line
when I get back.
No more buttermilk bread,
you can have ice cream instead,
and put those galoshes away
before my return, for when
I do I promise I'll stay
and clean up the mess
old Winter left in his wake.
May I suggest
you buy a new dress
and a sandal or two
for airing your toes.

Unstop a few bottles of wine,
white over red,
and Oh, what the heck,
offer the kids a sip
and hope they politely decline.
Now don't be impatient
and ask me to rush
for hasty is not my style.
I like to drop by
Like a favourite aunt who calls
on a favourite child,
in her pockets a special surprise.
I like to eavesdrop on you
a spell, put delight in your eyes
when you catch sight of me
saying hello on the wings
of a bird and its song.
I promise I'll be along
some day soon and I will
but you'll have to wait a bit.
I hope you don't mind.
And one more thing as you wait;
write me a song like
this one, all over the place
rhythm and rhyme,
slapped on a page with affection.
Nothing sublime."
It was morning.
That's all She said.
There was snow underfoot
and sun overhead
as I walked an agreeable mile.
Spring gave me her
calling card today.
It read, "I shall return."
And then She slipped away.

April

Watch your back!
This is no time
for long range planning!
Fickle April reinventing
the rules again. As the lion's
sudden surprise attack
shatters the very air,
She can ruin your day
unannounced or changing her mind
and yours, repair your
fragile hope with a sunny smile.

Watch your back! Ferocious and mild,
She won't give herself away.
She's randy and rowdy as March,
flirtatious and winsome as May.

May

As your maiden-like innocence
chaste as a novice
dreaming of taking
her ultimate vows,
tortures and torments
the heart to paralysis
aching for something
your heart can't allow.

So you scatter your petaline
blossoms around as you
mesmerize lovers
who long for your touch.
Drinking your perfume
they shamelessly hover
hopelessly hoping
despite your rebuffs.

As you call them to enter
your circle of dancing
whirling and laughing
beneath the warm sun,
you can never surrender
to whispers and glances
nor lie in one's arms
when the dancing is done.

You have cloistered the world
from its own discontentment,
glorified modesty,
chastened the night.
You arrive as a herald
docile, obedient,
the radiant bridesmaid,
the consort of light.

June

"North!" He commanded.
"North to the eye of Polaris.
Gallop you into the boreas,
imprison the darkness, awaken the dead.
Banish all that is Saturnine,
unburden the world-weary mind."

Helios thus in his kindness
lightly labours them forth,
coaxing, entreating them, "North, north
to the shadowless solstice."

Glorious Summer days,
garden of Summer smiles,
lovers and heart-heavy sighs
welcomed with sun-warmed praise.
Yours is the sun-gilt crown
of noon that goes round and round
luring the azure sky
into the sleeping hours.

There Summer's beauteous perfection
in lofty legend begotten
intoxicates creatures and man,
while the lingering sun
slumbers, his work being done.

At the chilling austral dawn
wheeling his coursers about,
Helios shatters the silence, "South!"

July

I wish I had dallied the longer,
risen a little earlier,
stretched out the limbs of the day
between blinkin and nod.
Put away labour and literature,
lifted my voice like a troubadour.
Begged Her to lead me astray
like a coquettish fraud.

I wish I had shamelessly plundered
her garden of earthly delights,
circled too close to the sun
against reason and odds.
Compromised virtue and wandered
the forbidden heat of the night,
but wishes are fraught with delirium
and bells are tolled.

I wished I had watched in the morning
her exotic weaving of veils
in her seemly mysterious silken
seduction of dawn.
Or cared not a fig for the warning
and drowned in her nights of champagne.
But I played the cautious tragedian.
Immobilized. Flawed.

August

I met a man upon the road
who asked me, "Why do you suppose
August is the best month of
the year?"

He changed his stride to bar my way
and were it not a pleasant day,
I might have thought him impudent
or queer.

Suffice to say my enterprise
what e'er it was did not prescribe
I sidle past as if he wasn't
there,

and being curious, truth be told,
I couldn't leave it unresolved
the mystery he determined
to declare.

"A little history," he explained.
"Augustus Caesar gave his name
to rest upon the eight month like
a crown.

He gave the month its majesty
and his name to posterity.
A clever bit of mischief you'll
allow.

I prize these little gems and rules
they don't teach in the modern schools.
These treasures that remind us of
the past."

He paused a length, and then he sighed,
a ghostly shadow crossed his eyes.
He took my arm, it was a feeble
grasp.

"So very many years ago
I don't recall, but this I know,
it was a sunny August after-
noon.

I came upon a mossy wall
near a field of golden corn,
thinking I might take a little
snooze.

Scarcely had I settled in
when I heard an awful din,
a motorcar had stopped to sound
its horn.

She rolled the window down and smiled,
'Could use some help if you've got time.
Come over to the farm tomorrow
morn.' "

'Tomorrow morn,' beneath his breath,
his voice was as the voice of death.
I drew back to review the road
beyond.

A lazy bend, a stony place,
what looked like a forgotten gate.
I made to say goodbye and carry
on.

He held his ground. "Before you leave,
those mornings were my 'joie de vivre.'
My heart was lighter than the summer
air.

And lost in the sublimity
of August' lush virility,
we fell in love, in love without
a care.

Her name was Mary Monaghan,
she called me 'Ted' her faithful man,
the answer to a wish she'd liked
to pray.

I worked the hours. Oh, how they fled.
We settled on a date to wed.
It had to be a glorious August
day."

I found my patience wearing thin
and tried not to encourage him
as he went on about his lengthy
yarn.

But he was on a mission now
and I didn't foresee how
his narrative could bring me any
harm.

I felt a dampish breeze arise.
I saw a welling in his eyes.
A grimace slowly crawled across
his face.

"Answer this," he growled at me,
"What is the tragic irony
of August? Did they teach you this
at school?

The war came tramping to my door.
The war they said would end all wars
began in August. And, and I
the fool,

took a gun and learned to march
patriotic, stiff as starch.
Told Mary she'd be my December
bride."

I felt as if I had been shot,
so shocking were his words and not
what I expected so I drew
aside

to piece together what he said,
to stay the spinning of my head.
Try to find some logic in
it all.

Another blast of wind and I
saw a whirl of dust blow by,
felt the temperature begin
to fall.

'Stay calm,' I said and calling on
my courage turned, but he was gone,
mindful of the gathering storm,
no doubt.

The village lay back there a mile.
I reasoned if I jogged a while
I could be indoors to wait
it out.

That's when I heard the coughing jar
of an antique motor car
cautioning its way around
the bend.

I watched it pull well off the road,
the driver in an overcoat
walk up to the gate and push
it in.

The figure stepped among the stones,
stooped, and laying something down,
turned to offer me a furtive
glance.

A roll of thunder bade me choose,
a dash for shelter or this new
development at which I stood
entranced.

But I was fixed upon the spot
and whether I had moved or not,
the heavens poured a great and sudden
rain.

All the landmarks far and near
all directions disappeared.
Standing here was neither loss
nor gain.

Then the torrent eased a spell,
eased enough for me to tell
where the car was parked and off
I went.

When at last I gained the bend
the storm was coming to an end
revealing yet a new
astonishment.

The car was just a heap of rust.
The driver vanished! Turned to dust!
I wondered should I laugh or should
I cry.

'Get out while the goings good,'
I told myself and yes, I would
have, only something else had caught
my eye.

The stony place behind the gate
a weed congested disarray,
turned out to be a cemetery
field.

Most of the markers were askew
or fallen down, except for two
almost upright, not as much
concealed.

This place was giving me the creeps!
I prayed to God to help me keep
my sanity as I approached
the spot.

To this very day, I swear,
I saw a clutch of flowers there,
out of season, fresh Forget-me-
nots.

I couldn't let it finish then.
I rubbed the mossy tablets when
some words or names or dates appeared
at last.

'Here lies Theodore 'Ted' McCabe
a corporal of the 10th. Brigade.
A wounded warrior carried home
to rest.'

I swept the other with my hand.
'Here lies Mary Monaghan
whose life was ended by a broken
heart.'

And that's not all, I found the dates
at the bottom of the slates.
They jumped out like an exclamation
mark.

They buried Ted on August third,
and Mary followed, take my word,
a fortnight onward of that fatal
year.

I went back later to that place
to learn or maybe just to trace
what happened but the memory's
unclear.

For ninety years have passed between
today and nineteen seventeen.
And August doesn't bring me
any cheer.

September

September courted me
and I the willing.
In garments soft and fair,
profuse and golden.
By fullness of her wealth,
her noble bearing,
She bade me to her arms
and did enchant me.

Her dowry overspills
with charm and treasure.
Across the blushing hills
She flaunts her pleasure.
In wholesomeness of form
she is maturing.
And beneath her azure shawl
She does her wooing.

Am I not flesh and blood?
Am I not easy?
She knew her hedon ways
would surely tease me.
As a poacher plies his stealth
by stream and garden,
I would steal her sweetest store
then beg her pardon.

September courted me
in her days of glory.
She bade me taste her fruit,
like the ancient story.
She promised sun and moon
And I the willing.
But her days are growing short.
And her nights are chilling.

October

How I envy him
this glorious afternoon
piloting his biplane over my porch.
The familiar unfamiliar 'Grrreee'
of the engine, the nonchalant
fabric wings wobbling along
like an infant taking its first steps,
tentative, confident, unable to stop,
loving the break-free from the ground,
the endless horizons, unlimited possibilities,
the up-there play of balances,
lift against gravity, drag versus propulsion.

How I wish to be his co-pilot someday,
wafting away on the warm October air,
my breath caught and held in awe of God's
ostentatious strut of emotional colours below,
delivered at last like a dancing leaf,
adrift in the cloudless blue.

Philistines!
Behind that line of trees
down the broken road.
The insistent repeat
of an air drill
returns like a nightmare.
Ack! Ack! Ack! Ack! Ack!

November

Under a stubborn fog-grey sky
November counts her thirty days.
Her aging winsome days and I
like sightless moths long gone astray,
search in vain for a flicker of light.

It seems the clouds have fallen to earth
and banished the edgings of shadow and line,
and the colours of things and the sound of mirth
and the sun and the moon and the passing of time,
'till moths and wanderers are numb and cold.

On some far sea shore there's a ship in distress.
In the woodlands creatures are shifting about.
November is neither at play or rest,
nor knows any welcome within or without
as She trundles along her cheerless course.

December

December is heavily on us,
(Oh, when did the Summer leave?)
snow filled skies and callous
winds this Solstice eve.
Fenceless fields meet shoulders
making the road disappear
where driving is an adventure
of white-knuckled fear.
"Mother of God, protect us,"
I whisper, and then
the scent of Summer roses
fills our van.

This is the land of dead things,
an inverse Sahara wind-
levelled, desolate, grim.
This is the desert called Winter.
I dream a dream of tomorrow
when Spring starts her journey north,
creeping with stealth as slow
as an indolent sloth.
I gaze at my white-crusted garden
and all I know
is the Summery crimson ramble
of roses below.

This is the land of dead things,
lost souls behind lost eyes
migrate to malls like wandering
tribes under cold desert skies.
I'll be content as a dreamer
left with the moon,
dreaming about a Redeemer
in his mother's womb.
As life sleeps under the cover
of Winter snows,
His birth arrives like the hope
of a perfumed rose.

Ice Storm In April

First came the great grey drapes
of hail followed by sky-sprayed
freezing rain. Then hail again
and another swath of shivering rain.
By mid morning the street
was pebbled marzipan, a curling sheet
from house to house.

Save for a few befuddled birds
working the crystalline grass, nothing stirred.
The world and its chaos and toil
was cancelled today, its turmoil
encased in a transient transparent shell
like a frozen unexploded bomb
waiting to be unearthed.

And so, my love, let us re-invent
warmth in this cold house, transcend
all things counter, contrived by nature
or man, while that transpicuous conjuror
undertakes to consign to the grave
irrepressible Spring, our fears allay
to the sun's caress.

Some Psalms

Blessings That Fall
(psalm 128)

Which child is favoured most? You bid me tell.
Learned Brendan wrestling with his soul?
Nuala wholly wrapt in motherhood?
Nay-defying Niamh, that self propelled
lady? Roisin patiently unfolding
like a flower? Maybe her many moods
advances Bridget's charm above the rest.
Or is it Ciarán's freedom from pretense?
Or Turlough's tug of war with youth and power?
A father's love is neither more or less
apportioned by degrees of difference.
He thanks God for his children every hour,
but for his wife, he thanks Him every breath.

Ravens Who Cry
(psalm 147)

Regard the flight of the ignoble crow;
ungraceful, awkward, plodder of the air,
like a black blot against any sky
until he finds his pulpit on a post.
Then, head into the wind, shoulders square,
he coughs his raucous caw-caw-cophony
into the dawn. This disharmonious voice
crying in the urban wilderness
a monosyllabic message to the world.
This unwelcome disturber of the peace
sings his Master's praise for all he's worth.
Unmoved by his simplicity of words,
unfettered by the discard of his race.

These Are Like Chaff
(psalm 1)

What omens grieve the trees around my house?
Almond, lilac, cherry, once arrayed
in blooms that blushed upon the face of Spring.
Leaf-lean maples generations old
where red and yellow singing birds endured
the chattering of apprehensive squirrels
waiting for the chestnut and its friends
to yield their fruit. Alas! I fear their doom.
Men of science scramble to account
and speak of shifting winds and global trends.
Forgetful of you, Lord, have we assumed
a harvest of afflictions? Brought about
this melancholy murmuring of trees?

Made By Your Fingers
(psalm 8)

Into Eden's garden I was born,
from common clay and spittle have I sprung.
My father and my mother made my flesh
a vessel imaging the perfect form
of the Creator, the most Holy One.
I am the lord of Eden! I possess
and I subdue all things that I survey
across the sky, beneath the yielding waves.
And all that walk, walk as my will commands.
See how I am poised this very day
to realign the heavens that You gave.
I, 'though less than god but more than man,
have full embraced the splendour of my pride.

All Have Turned Aside
(psalm 14)

At first they drove You from the living womb,
then told You to go wait beyond the door.
Your name was stricken from the wedding list,
your image was too counter to the norm.
The fools said to themselves, "For evermore
there is no God, for God has been dismissed!"
The hour approaches fast, the hour of fear
when ignorance becomes their shield for blame,
when they will agonize that You are gone
and call Your name, demanding You appear
to rescue them from danger, to explain.
And You will give them cause to think upon
the Gentleman who heard and stayed away.

Lift Me Up
(psalm 69)

Through rain-smeared windows all day long I've tried
in vain to find a point of clarity.
In here I'm warm and dry and safe and still.
All things beyond are warped as heaven cries
upon a world lamenting on its knees
a pagan prayer to guard against its ills;
"Deliver us from SARS, from terror bombs,
from deadly stings, from soaring costs, from truth.
Save us from ourselves." But who will save?
The judge? The politician? Soldiers? Mobs?
And then I felt, as if I needed proof,
across these infirm limbs, a sudden wave
of grace by which a single soul is won.

People Who Refuse
(psalm 95)

On Friday afternoon we rented ice
for children full of energy and dreams:
he scored the winning goal in overtime,
her flawless program earned a golden prize.
"Reach for the sky!" "Dare to live your dreams."
"Be all you can and more, the world is thine!"
These are the signs that greet them at the door,
but as they leave there's no one there to say,
"Thanks, friend." "Well done!" "We'll miss your friendly
    smile."
This generation took the bait and swore
an oath unto itself, "I'll go my way
alone, I don't need God. I have a style."
And who will pay the rent when we are gone?

The Plains Of Nations
(psalm 33)

This is no time for the faint of heart.
This most ungodly time. This foul epoch
a Culture, said the Holy Man, of Death.
A providential man needs live apart
or haunted by the crowing of a cock.
His trust in God assures him not to fret
as scheming men of nations unified
by fear, strike His name from their very mouths.
Like exiles in a darkened bitter land,
we wait upon the coming of Springtide
when doors will burst asunder, stopped tongues shout
the sacred name of the Creator and
the dawning of His Golden Age of Life!

The Bread Of Tears
(psalm 80)

Around the marbled corners empty men
mutter empty mantras of defeat,
or sleep like pre-born children wrapped inside
a plastic sack. Survival here depends
on two things, the pity of the street
and whether Winter's breath is harsh or kind.
Above, the pleated skirt and Saville Row
panhandlers hustle for a bigger buck.
Survival here depends on market trends,
the fragile fix of stocks and bonds and gold.
Once, a man of troubled heart mistook
a nod for love, and thought he felt it mend
the pity of his empty hungry soul.

Lords Of The Whole World
(psalm 45)

My heart is stirred to see you walk with him,
the man you love within whose eyes you shine
like a jewel set in gold, like as a queen.
He is your husband now, he is your king,
for you have given cause for God to smile
on you with gladness when, O happy scene!
you called on Him to witness holy vows.
Today the years ahead rise and appear
as vague as morning mist across the lake.
But heaven starts to sing your praises now
and whispers them in your beloved's ear,
"I had a dream. I dreamed that l was an
old man. I had a son and I was happy."

Impotent Mutterings
(psalm 2)

It reads like this: the W.H.O.,
G-7, U.N., N.A.F.T.A.,
the E.U. and the W.M.F.,
C.I.A., K.G.B., N.A.T.O.
These and others like them like to say
God couldn't take the pressure so He left.
Oh, you foolish, foolish, foolish men!
When all your foolish bickering is stopped,
is this where you retreat, the common ground
you all agreed to when your quest began?
Then ask yourselves, you godless and corrupt,
is this world better than the one you found?
He's throwing back His head and how He laughs!

Voice Like Fire
(psalm 18)

As of old when Yahweh's voice was heard
Thundering from the heavens' heaving skies
Bringing mighty massifs to their knees,
Seabeds from their stupor disinterred,
Consuming like an all-consuming fire
The enemies of those who sang His praise,
So will it be tomorrow! No mistake!
His patience has, His patience has run out.
He hears the disenfranchised of our times,
The desecration of his holy day,
The silent voices. These are not without
His justice when He lets his arrows fly
Tomorrow as of old when He was heard.

To See Ourselves
(psalm 19)

Who can detect the failings of his heart?
See himself as only God can see?
Flush out his hidden faults as on the tide?
My brother, I shall speak my own behalf
As one acquainted with inconsistency,
The constant push against primeval pride,
The fear of God's judicious eye and true.
And how will you, your backers and your kin
Explain yourselves when all our sins exposed
Before our eyes, that odious turpitude
We harbour in our souls imprisoning
Us in death, erupt? God only knows
The fate that we deserve. The fate we own.

Questions And Answers
(psalm 15)

Any man who asks, "What must I do
to be saved?" Sincerity and truth
or, "I don't need to know, but just in case,"
behind the thought, deserves at least to know.
Sometimes when I walk my Winter route,
staggering through the snow, wind in my face,
everything in me wants to call it quits.
Love the God who made you, and that guy
next door who never says hello,
give him a break and patiently persist.
Often strolling under Summer skies,
sun in my face, my faith in You restored,
I tell myself, "I can. I can do this."

The Godless Ones
(psalm 53)

Before the puck is dropped at centre ice;
"Please rise and join in the singing of
our national anthem." The super star
begins, "O Canada….we see thee rise,
the true North strong and free….love keep our land"…..
No one seemed to notice the faux pas.
After all, she's such a lovely girl.
Was this slipshod breach of etiquette
or God dismissed for getting in the way?
And there I stood, dumbstruck, a sanctus bell
hole still as they sign off Your sacredness.
How would that look on a resumé?
References: my fans. They worship me.

Baseness Stands High
(psalm 12)

Juxtaposed these two words stand apart.
Vile, contemptible, in value low.
Superior in character and kind.
The psalmist might have been an avant-garde
scribe for God's then-and-forever code.
I imagine he would have allowed a smile.
I imagine as he worked in haste, inspired
not wishing to misplace a single word,
obedient to his master's oracle,
that he missed the clever paradigm
at first. But when his balance was restored,
foresaw the writ of wisdom carry on
from age to age for topsy-turvy man.

Let Me Sing
(psalm 13)

I love the songs that sing of simple gifts.
Rewarding days of work, slow nights of rest,
a home to come home to, an easy birth,
the cheer to give a faltering side a lift,
this life that I might serve You at my best
before my mortal shackles fall to earth.
I have lived to witness in a span
of time, my fellows faltering along
the road in search of tunes to ease the pain
of broken spirits, grief endured and, "Damn
it all, I don't know what it is I've
done wrong! Is it my fault? Am I to blame?"
I know that road. I know it all to well.

Tongues So Smooth
(psalm 5)

You know them. You've seen them a hundred times.
The smooth talkers. Your new best friend, his hand
perfectly weighed on your shoulder, light
but firm. His practiced words. His perfect crime.
And you, his new accomplice, understand
you're being had but love his lovely lies.
They lie in wait for those who want to trust
that all men have the benefit of a doubt.
Oh God, who knows the ways of evil men,
let evil destroy evil as it must.
Call them forth and hold them to account
in your own time. But in the interim
don't forget your friends who fret and sigh.

Rest Secure
(psalm 4)

Courage, either personal or known
to all, is easy to facilitate
when chasing after lies or self-deceit.
After all, who dares to speak his own
mind aloud when politic and state
engage and claim the right to his conceit.
Find courage in the heart of he who lifts
his eyes to heaven praying for relief,
in the voices now praising Him who hears
the call, who hears the call and sends the gift
of peace that all the world can scarce believe.
At the end of the day, he has no fears
and sleeps courageous as a mother's child.

When Foundations Fall
(psalm 11)

When fire and brimstone from the olden days
struck the mighty towers of Babel down,
they did not see the counsel in the ash.
Traders who had many fortunes made
mourned the city ruined within the hour
and for a time, some went stumbling back
to find in God an answer for their loss.
Now that the dust is swept away like bad
dreams and memories, and virtuous men
dismissed for lack of worth, the endless lust
for fortune's favour insinuates the land
again, in bold defiance of heaven's
holy throne. And how the winds do howl!

You Have Heard

(psalm 6)

We prayed the Rosary one night with two
friends who said afterwards, "You are our
only friends." Later I thought it odd,
but on reflection decided it might be true.
Except for them and but a handful more,
our list of friends is short who call on God.
One day a neighbour said that we were seen
as that eccentric family down the block.
I heard the penny fall. And I recalled
the crossing of the street midway, the mean-
spirited exclusion from events, the talk.
The talk that makes a little village small.
But we're still here, and You still hear us pray.

Lex Talionis

(psalm 7)

Signs on subway walls that read like this,
"The bad news, God is dead. The good news, you
don't need him," proclaim how very lost
and isolated is the atheist's
disposition and his point of view.
He hopes that God lives and being righteous,
slow to anger, just, and all that stuff,
recognizes the hidden plea for help.
That he, the denier, is overlooked
in his spitefulness. That's there's enough
(a tiny drop of) mercy being withheld
to bail him out. This comes from one who took
the time to smear his name with fingers crossed.

Encuigries

1

Why ask me?
Heavens above!
How can I define
friendship? A flame of mine
called it the coward in love.

2

The North wind
cried, "Who defies
my might? Who dares try
me?" Sweetly in reply
violet, "It is I."

3

Suppose God
called you by name
today, would you be
disquieted? At ease?
Ask me how I'd hide my shame.

4

Does your soul
remember life
before birth? Mine does.
Listen. Be silent. Close
your eyes. Don't you know that voice?

5

Joy starts here
in the heart's heart.
Aren't men created
equal? Whence this hatred
that drives sons of God apart?

6

Instantly!
Thus God forgives.
Ours is a process.
Is that clear to you? Yes?
Thus is the saintly life lived.

7

Two questions!
Not one or three?
One's answer can wait.
Two cry out for debate.
And three? Three spread anarchy

8

Paper route.
Weekly income.
Same old, same old news.
Does it not comfort you?
Give you courage to press on?

9

What? My prize
Hypoestes
stripped by spider mites!
Don't drop your jaw in fright.
Can't I hate these____ing pests?

10

Where are you
birds and Spring? Where
your glorious songs
proclaiming hope at dawn?
Hush, my heart. Stay your despair.

11
In dreams our
encounters beg
the question; which most
shapes us, real or remote?
Comes first the chicken or the egg?

12
Empty words
dispassionate
and yes, even cold
soon make your love grow old.
Can't your eyes speak? Charm and bait?

13
That French girl
in the kitchen
Musée; did she hear
me gasp when she came near?
Ou était ma discrétion?

14
What's that line?
Do you forget?
(This humanity,
buffoons of me, me, me).
"Stop the world, I want to get"..........

15
My true love
prefers moonbeams.
I am morning's man.
What, pray tell, is her plan?
A rendevouz in our dreams?

16

This day, God's
gift to you. Non-
renewable. Free.
Do you know what I mean?
Give Him thanks before its gone?

17

Where is God?
Is He cellared
in your heart like some
secret shameful thing? Come,
let us discover His stars.

18

Who knows where
time goes? Gone. Quick
as a wink. No wild
guess? Try God's "Mankind" files.
See: Behaviours. Comedic.

19

God, a sense
of humour? Somehow
I think so. Visit
your mirror. Look in it.
I ask you, who is laughing now?

20

Ponder this;
Which is worse?
A fragile conscience
or full faith in science?
Each by the other is cursed.

21

On the trails
strangers' faces
coming towards me. Must
we pass in shared distrust?
Would a smile arrest our pace?

22

Wired for sound.
Stone-faced. Eyes down
or sun-glassed. Silent.
What is it you present?
How can I invert that frown?

23

Have I lied
to you before?
Question all they say.
Trust yourself. Now. Today.
Have I lied to you before?

24

Queen Anne's lace.
Weed indeed! Strong.
Regal. Fancy free.
(How can the rose compete?)
Can all her suitors be wrong?

25

Everything!
I want to know
everything. Let's try
these two for starters: Why
must it be? Why was it so?

26

Do you call
Time your ally
or your enemy?
Perhaps Time lacks worth, being free.
But suppose you had to buy?

27

Braggart! Your
memory serves
you well! Did she say
"Yes" or "No?" Did you phrase
the question as she deserves?

28

Graffiti
on toilet walls
compels me enquire,
who put it there? And why?
Let' see. "For a good time call"…..

29

You! Must you
abuse lines from
Literature all
the time? This above all?
To thine own self be true. Done.

30

Can the love
of God be swerved?
A loving parent's
patience is never spent.
Nag. Nag. Nag. Is God perturbed?

31
Mango fruit,
before you eat,
are they red or green
or yellow? How to clean
stringy fibres from your teeth?

32
Who says there's
global warming?
If I have cold feet,
and fear to face defeat,
aren't will and ill conspiring?

33
Here's the rub;
does being what
we eat require a
boorish diet? Or can
we choose between 'cool' and 'hot?'

34
Will you tell
me what is truth?
Should it be spoken
or heard? I say breaking
a promise exposes truth.

35
"Please!" She begged.
"Do you love me?"
Your familiar shrug.
"Isn't it enough that
you agreed to share my bed?"

36
You! Asking
to talk about
God? How can that be?
You cannot speak to me
without causing pain or doubt.

37
In the street
or country lane?
Does peace need a place
to reside? There is space
in heart's eternal refrain.

38
Canada?
Too North for me!
We have cloud and snow
and it's fifteen below.
What did you expect, palm trees?

39
Why should age
keep you from me?
Which improves with time,
fresh milk or vintage wine?
Poured, they adapt equally.

40
Is it so
hard? Making each
day Thanksgiving Day?
Whether at work or play
grace is never out of reach.

41

Please. Thank you.
Sorry. It's my
fault. Yes ma'am. No sir.
What happened to these words?
When did civility die?

42

Don't you love
Fall? The corn flake
crunch of leaves, golden
fields and moons, abundance
gone mad. Want to celebrate?

43

Here's what I
don't understand;
are there that many
daft eaters? Sugar free.
Salt free. What do they mean? Bland!

44

Afterwards,
if I agree
to put the seat down,
(why that skeptical frown?)
will you lift it up for me?

45

Good news? Bomb
kills ten. More porn
on TV. Jobless
increase. Good news? Rejoice!
Unto us a child is born.

46

A light shines
(our eyes are dim)
in the darkness (we
cannot see). Do you fear
His mercy? Misconceive Him?

47

What is it
that really haunts
our hearts? Torments
on cold Winter nights? Il
est née le divine enfant.

48

If kings bring
gifts and angels
sings, why can't we? Come,
let us adore Him. Come.
Is He not Emmanuel?

49

Oh, blest babe!
Oh, holy night!
Who among us can
resist a child? What man
turns away from love's pure light?

50

Don't you love
hymns and carols?
Could it be Winter's
air held music better
when God's choir sang their heralds?

51
Ciarán did
you know? You smile
a secret smile. Tell
me that story again.
Did you know Mary's boy child?

52
What thoughts or
passions define
an angel? Free will
applied, does he know sin?
What grace! A soul without pride!

53
But you give
yourself away
every time. You loathe
"Goodbye," don't you? Suppose
I don't like, "Have a nice day?"

54
I say ban
zero degrees!
This needs some mending.
Is there 'worth' to 'nothing?'
Does 'no' degrees melt or freeze?

55
The Freedom
of Choice Act is
secured. Damn them all!
Whose freedom? What choice? Call
me naïve as a foetus.

56
Do you know
what comes after
loss of morals? Pass?
"The fish will be the last
one to discover water."

57
Remember
Summer suppers?
Great food, heady wine.
Weren't those the best of times?
Let's go get some steak and beer.

58
My heart, my
solitary
heart held in my hands
without shame. Silence? And
pray tell, where does that leave me?

59
Lord, you are
hard on lovers.
How long must I wait
for your compassionate
touch? Shed tears for your pleasure?

60
Really? We
call on fewer
muscles to smile than
to frown? This small human
act yields more growth than manure!

61
What is this
Big Bang theory?
What exactly 'Banged?'
I know. God clapped His hands
delighted by you and me.

62
We've heard it
said man's work or
play defines his 'self.'
How do you see yourself?
Are you simply behaviour?

63
Think about
eternity
and your head will spin
and spin. Does it begin
and end? Are you asking me?

64
Red wine. Blue
skies. Your embrace.
Other joys. What's the
point? What's the agenda?
This life is an awesome place!

65
Did Joseph
make Jesus toys?
Is that all they saw
in underwhelming awe,
an old man and a young boy?

66

What are these
so called Human
Rights Commissions? If
they're not 'thought police' stiffs,
what is their real purpose then?

67

And you, my
beauty, is yours
skin deep? It's a trick
question. What do I think?
I'm always, always sincere.

68

You're looking
for flattery
aren't you? If its words
you seek, I've got words. Words
are cheap. Where's your dignity?

69

Who can solve
the enigma
found in this river
island? Which is better,
shrine or shroud? We must go back.

70

Off the boat
from Montmagny,
which response comes first;
softer footfall or burst
of tears? How else to meet Grosse-ile?

71

How many
lie beneath these
rolling mounds? Why do
no birds sing? Sadness blooms
here like a garden of weeds.

72

What prayer
is most often
heard by God? At least
from this old soul it is.
Surrender? Think 'fallen man.'

73

Do you know
about life's 'Best
before' date? Listen,
there is an extension
plan. Want it? Give more. Take less.

74

When, alas
love redefines,
how will you behave?
Will you remain a slave
to lust, or sing like fine wine?

75

Sundays. The
Deck. Good wine. Food.
And great poetry.
Do you recall? Make me
proud once more. Bashful? Not you.

76
Egg. Larva.
Pupa. Adult.
Who would want this life?
Who would pay such a price?
Ah, butterfly. How you float.

77
"How do I
love thee?" She penned.
I can't quantify
love, nor would ever try.
What if I don't understand?

78
Answer this;
what is Beauty?
It is every poet's
pursuit. But you know, don't
you? Where God goes, there goes She.

79
Blurted out,
"My faith is gone."
Now what? Should we say
"All is lost?" Not today.
Never. Hope springs eternal.

80
Why have our
children fallen
away from their faith?
They're not rich. They don't hate
anyone. What, then, changed them?

81

Do you greet
mornings in prayer?
As for me, I would
be unsynchronized should
I not. And when you retire?

82

Have you not
heard the good news?
Two new saints, one Spring.
One Pope canonizing
two Popes. Why? Heaven approves.

83

What do child
'experts' want when
they help them to play?
Want to know what I say?
think social engineering.

84

I sliced through
the hot muffin
for my grandchild. "See
the steam?" He surprised me,
"Like Thomas the Tank Engine?"

85

What six words
most warm my heart?
Simple honest words
sadly less often heard,
"Can I have an up Grandpa?"

86
Your first kiss,
how did it go?
Do I remember
Mine? Trembling heart. Puckered
lips. I crashed across her nose.

87
My grandchild
played with her life.
Why weren't we informed?
And if she came to harm,
however should we reply?

88
When it stings
the honeybee
dies. Does it 'know' this?
Does it sacrifice its
life for the hive willingly?

89
What has turned
Russia's heart? Might
she save the world from
itself while the West bans
Alpha and Omega life?

90
Canada,
a moral slew!
How did this happen?
We took paper and pen
and wrote the rules. What's your view?

91

Apps. ipods.
Tablets. Cell phones.
Don't kids play outside
these days? Didn't you cry,
laugh, win, lose, bloody your nose?

92

Where did you
get your great smile?
Who taught you the creed
of generosity?
See who's blushing all the while.

93

Who saw this
coming? A Jew
who would call Jesus
the Messiah, not just
a prophet? Who knew? He knew.

94

In Rhodes Greece
an icon weeps,
St. Michael in tears.
Should humanity fear?
Comes the night thief as we sleep?

95

Fires. Droughts. Floods.
Storms. Do you think
the Earth's gone mad? Or
could it be (I shudder!)
more signs Apocalyptic?

96

Why are our
bishops tight-lipped?
The ship flounders at
sea, the crew lazy, fat,
confused. How long must we drift?

97

You who love
to act, to write,
think on this; which need
most arises? Feeding
your muse or a goodly wife?

98

When may one
tell a white lie?
"Grandpa, what's that thing
for making Mommies sing?"
Disbelief flashed before her eyes.

99

At day's end
I wonder, do
you welcome sleep? Fear
and guilt, that wretched pair
destroy sleep. Did I assume?

100

Can it be
true? Pianist
found guilty of noise
pollution! My oh my!
What could be less sound than this?

WHIMSEY

How Tea Saved The Irish Race

She used to say,
"Tea is the sustenance
of the Irish," my mother.
"Tea and porridge."
She got that from Mary
my hard-boiled aunt
who poured boiling water
along with a largish

measure of tea leaves
into another pot to be boiled.
"Tea should be thick enough
for a mouse to dance on."
My aunt frightened me.
She hardly ever smiled
and had a smoker's cough
that rasped like a hack saw.

I thought she ate bits
of nails with her oatmeal
and put iron filings
into her tea. Uncle Ned
was her exact antithesis.
He was a more spiritual
and philosophical human being.
This is what he said

about drinking tea: "Tea
is a soothing libation
best enjoyed with a friend.
It grew in the Garden
of Eden. You see,
our very salvation
need not have depended
on Christ's crucifixion.

"If Adam and Eve had
invented tea instead
of original sin, the devil
himself would have
brought bread and jam."
A wise man, my Uncle Ned,
his eyes always a-twinkle,
always good for a laugh.

Our house was a magnet
for rumours, runaways,
favours and freeloaders.
My mother a soft touch,
usually without regret.
Night or day
she opened her door
to the blest and cursed.

Tea was her balm
and her tongue stirred
the pot. "Come here, alanna.
You saw him at the pictures
with another girl? Calm
down now, not another word.
That feckin' blackguard!
You're much better than her

and too good for him.
I'll put the kettle on."
Another time: "Missus,
me Mam wants the loan
of a fag and some
tea. Me Da's drunk again."
"Of course darlin'." Then hiss,
"That man's a right arsehole."

Once she'd baked a birthday
cake for me when
the door opened and a neighbour
sauntered in. My mother rose
to fill the pot with tea.
"You've been baking again.
That's a grand cake, sure.
I don't suppose….?"

"The tea's gone cold."
My mother's smile was soft.
But when she'd gone,
"I was too polite.
I should have told
her outright to feck off!
She's as bold as brass, that one.
A brazen little shite."

When I was a kid
I ate porridge and bread
and jam and birthday cake,
always washed down
by tea. If Uncle Ned
was right when he said
tea could have saved
our immortal souls, now

what would have happened
to the Irish race?
We'd all be right
as rain; my aunt,
mother, uncle sadly bland.
Nobody put in their place.
No "feckin' arseholes" or "shites."
Only coffee drinking sods!

Aphrodisiacs

The Romans thought the apple
an aphrodisiac. At one end
the still intact maiden blossom,
the bell curved vulva at the other
penetrated by a shaft of wood.
The innocence and experience of desire,
blushing skin, fruit of love,
the Romans thought the apple.

A beetle *lytta vesicatoria,*
powdered, introduced by slight
of hand into a lady's drink
for one purpose; it might
arouse her sexual desire,
stimulate the feminine libido,
or, having strychnine, kill her,
the beetle *lytta vesicatoria.*

Bananas with honey and coffee
taken daily, liberally by some
(not me, I repeat, not me)
seeking an energized "wumph!"
or the like, offer visual,
tactile support, colour shape,
promises steamy and full
coffee with bananas and honey.

Raw oysters and champagne!
Well! Here's the scene:
candlelight, music, for two,
open mouth, tongue sucking in
whole slippery plump raw flesh,
then bubbly cascading wine,
dizziness, laughter, a bed of fresh
raw oysters and champagne.

Chocolate and cinnamon spices
taken alone or together
bring sweet, bittersweet, sighs
amorous between him and her,
brown mouth kisses,
"Oohs" and "Aahs," sticky fingers
and other such blisses,
chocolate and cinnamon spices.

Potions and perfumes and paint,
wanton weapons of sin
leave a man bewildered,
wondering what door he came in.
She is the prowling predator,
he is the meal
rapt in the heavy air
of perfume and potions and paint.

A garlicky onion sauté
with its simmering savour,
ambrosial racy bouquet
leaves all the others adrift
on the sea of banal.
This is not delicate fare.
Anticipation is crucial, crucial
with garlic and onions sautéed.

Sautéed onions and garlic's
redolent, saucy layers
invade our sensual souls.
Look at the golden veneer
glistening there, hear them
simmer pleasures and promises,
inhale the luscious alluvium
of onions and garlic sautéed.

A garlic and onions sauté
opens the portals of desire,
piques the amorous appetite,
massage as with tender fire
flights of fanciful lust.
A sudden odoriferous spray
can buckle the knees,
garlic and onions sautéed.

A sauté of onions and garlic
salivates sex
now and for the rest of the day.
The lingering incense vexes
desires to frustration
if not relieved anon.
Beware the alluring invitation,
the sautéed garlicky onion fixation.

The Ballad of Andy and Niamh

being a brief history of their courtship
and a glimpse into their future.

The Meeting

I went down to the Goderich fair
as I had done so oft' before,
to dance for all the people there
and stroll along Lake Huron's shore.

And when the night had taken hold
and I was beckoned to the strand,
I came upon a handsome bold
musician from a foreign land.

I couldn't understand his speech
but from the twinkle in his eye
I knew that on this August beach
I'd found myself another toy.

> "Look what I've got.
> He thinks I'm hot.
> I'll be adored
> until I'm bored.
> This is his fate
> and I'm not ready for a mate."

The next three days were like a whirl
of song and dance and heady wine.
I let him think I was his girl,
at least so long as he was buying.

And then one evening very late,
those little hours before sunrise,
we met along a darkened street,
me Mam and Daddy, quelle surprise!

Something happened there to me.
My mind went blank, my mouth went dry.
I searched for answers, could it be
that I was falling for this guy?

"Look what I've got.
He thinks I'm hot.
Of course that's true,
but he's cute too.
My parents' eyes
have always seen right through my lies."

The Decision

Confusion is a foggy friend
who clouds the mind and heart with fear,
who smothers with bewilderment
each vain attempt to see things clear.

I don't remember driving home.
My car must have a sense of space.
How I arrived, God only knows.
I think His angels kept me safe.

I fell into a nine day prayer
to seek discernment for my life.
And he went off to Combermere
in contemplation of a wife.

"Look what I've got.
He thinks I'm hot?
He passed the sham
for what I am.
He makes me whole,
he looks into my secret soul."

The Commitment

Eight months have vanished like a sigh,
events have swept our lives apace.
We've crossed the ocean several times.
We've made new plans, the bills kept pace.

Today we took our holy vows
and sealed them with our marriage rings.
I've got him in my clutches now!
He chased me but I caught him!

I know it's just an old cliché
to think we've only just begun.
He wants four kids, I want eight.
But if it hurts we'll stop at one.

"Look what we've got.
We know we're hot.
My man alive,
his buxom bride.
We both are blessed
so we'll leave God to do the rest."

The Ballad of Bridget and Terry

There's a story I've been told
about a man named Terry Gole,
about his honey Bridget Myers
and how their courtship did transpire.

Now Robin and his merry men
came to Elmira's festival
chasing wenches, drinking mead
in the Spring of double O three.

He was a muddy monkey man,
a travelling clown, I understand.
She was herald to this fair
and made announcements here and there.

When mingling among the crowd
he heard a voice both strong and loud.
She saw him in his pigpen plight,
love didn't blossom at first sight.

> Quelle dommage,
> It's such a shame.
> Peut-être la romance
> is in vain.
> The herald
> et le chimpanzee
> had failed tomber
> in love that day.

Imagine Summer in your mind
and they beside The Tooth of Time,
Terry telling her, "I'll bet
you'd like to see my chemistry set.

"Come to my lab, close the door
and see my H2SO4.
And here's something you'll like a lot,
my Bunsen Burner's really hot."

"I don't like games," she said, "I don't.
Don't try to fool me 'cause you won't.
But as I do like older men,
perhaps you'd like to try again."

They seemed to work things out at last.
A job in Afghanistan passed.
And tired of hearing him complain,
she stopped picking at her nails.

       It's wonderful,
       c'est merveilleux,
       both are happy,
       tous les deux.
       He needs a job,
       cherche un emploi.
       She needs a stage,
       applaudissements!

One Maple Villa dinner night
here was Terry so polite,
schmoozing Bridget's Daddy and
asking for her marriage hand.

Some time later from that place,
he sent her on a wild goose chase,
from bowling green to mews to park
with roses as a guiding mark

that lead her to a red canoe,
across the river, that will do.
'Cause Terry's waiting on the shore
with, "Be my bride forevermore."

Now Terry has his Missus G,
another bro-in-law for me.
And Bridget's got a sporting role...
she just can't wait to score a Gole!

Yes, they're in love,
comme "Je t'adore,"
with each other,
comme "Je t'adore."
Cherchez un lit,
come shut the door.
We'll make our own
histoire d'amour.

A Place To Call Her Own

Before the master lifts his head,
before cold Winter's night has fled,
before the house its sleep has shed,
the hired maid has left her bed
and gone downstairs alone.

She's fanned the embers into flame,
she's poured the water from the pail,
she's drawn the tea, always the same,
she's heard the mistress call her name
and answered with a groan.

The day becomes its own routine;
the meals are set, the tables cleaned,
the floors are swept, and in between
the laundry loads are boiled clean
the dried around the stove.

There's no joy to be sought or won,
there is no youth, her youth is gone.
There's only work, work on and on,
there is no dream to dream upon
a place to call her own.

That was a hundred years ago.
That was a life a maid might know
that gave her neither bliss nor woe.
That was, that is this house, but, Oh!
Her presence is still known.

Free from that North-East corner room.
Free, like a spirit from her tomb.
Free from the years of gloom and gloom.
Free to renew, to flower, to bloom,
and through these halls to roam.

Now in her gown of aura'd light,
now in her Summer of delight,
now she presents a pleasant sigh,
now as we to her invite
a welcome to this home

where every traveller finds a stay,
where laughter's music lifts the day,
where children's quarrels rise and sway,
wherein life winds its merry way
and dreamers are reborn.

It's here our daily lives are told
and here where Bridget's youth unfolds
here, in her room, but not in scold,
called in the early morn.

Teasing, her brother whispers low
teasingly out of reach, and so
these little games play to-and-fro
testing the other's will to go
down the backstairs alone.

In silence she stalks on silent feet,
silently steps where floorboards creak,
silently measuring every beat.
The silent deception nearly complete,
and then she hears a moan.

Only the wind, she justifies,
only an echo in her mind.
Only the wind. Was that a sigh?
Slowly she turns to look behind.
It chills her to the bone!

Then, when a heartbeat has its rest,
then are a hundred years compressed.
Then fears dissolves to tenderness
when then is now, when guest meets guest
each in the other's home.

Two maidens on a timeless stairs,
two maidens understanding there's
a maiden's place, one here, one there.
Two maidens drawn through time to share
a place to call her own.

The Ballad of Ciarán, Destroyer Of Bed!

The room is so cosy
where I spend my day,
where afternoon sunlight
can visit and play
with dinosaur monsters
that stalk on the walls,
while I in my frame
snuggle safely and warm.

I'd stay here forever,
no, really, I would!
My roommate is friendly,
the animals good,
but when the day's over
the one thing I dread
is the coming of Ciarán,
Destroyer of Bed!

Now Turlough his brother
is any bed's treat.
The lower bunk's his
and he goes straight to sleep
with his head on his pillow
and him curled up small,
he lies still and comfy
'till way past the dawn.

But Ciarán has never
shown me such respect.
I know he's determined
to make me a wreck!
His Mommy and Daddy
think he's here to rest,
but I know he isn't,
that sneaky blond pest!

He'll kiss them goodnight,
close his eyes and pretend
that he's already halfway
to slumberland, then,
with the door tightly shut
and the light switches dimmed,
a strange transformation
will come upon him.

This sweet daytime cherub,
this dear halo'd head
becomes Mighty Ciarán!
Destroyer of Bed!

My job is to give him
a comfortable sleep.
He comes here to crush me,
that bed-bashing creep!

First to go is my beautiful
quilt from the top.
He rolls and he rolls
'till it falls with a "flop!"

Next the bed sheet which
all day I've kept straight and neat,
is kicked, squished and lumpified
down to his feet!

Now he turns to the left
then three more to the right
and my favourite blanket
slides out of sight.

My mattress is hammered
and bitten and squeezed.
He elbows it, smucks it
and still isn't pleased.

For me it's a nightmare,
a terrible dread.
I wish he would bunk
with his brother instead.

But Ciarán's a bed wrecking
veteran, it's true.
He beats me each night
leaving me black and blue!

My worst fear is simple,
one morning I'll bet,
I'll wake up to find
that my pillow's been 'et!'

I don't understand
why he does this to me.
If he'd snooze lying still
then I'd happier be.

But I'll be here nightly
until it is said
that I outlasted Ciarán,
Destroyer of Bed!

Leprechauns

When I woke up this morning,
my feet felt a little cold.
A shiver crawled over my shoulders,
the bed covers lay on the floor.

I thought that this was peculiar,
I usually sleep so sound.
Perhaps I had been dreaming
and was tumbling round and round.

But when I stepped out for the bathroom
something made me to stop,
it wasn't what I expected
and I froze on the very spot!

Beside my soft bunny slippers
the carpet was slightly wet.
I know I wasn't mistaken,
the evidence is there yet.

I dressed and I opened the curtains
and gazed at the beautiful sight
of the first snowfall of Winter.
It filled me with childish delight.

The sparkling blue sky and the morning
were calling me outside to play,
and racing downstairs and the hallway
I opened the door to the day.

The garden was covered with frosting,
the statues wore pointed white hats.
A nervous black squirrel from a treetop
was scolding a neighbourhood cat.

A mischievous breeze in the cedars
tickled a bough full of snow.
It slid with a 'flump' down the branches
and frightened two sparrows below.

The scene was just like a postcard
painted with delicate care;
glimmering, shimmering, diamonds,
tingling cold crisp air.

I thought of the kitchen and breakfast
and turned to reach for the door,
that's when I noticed the footprints,
three pair of them, what's more!

One set was very much human,
in that there was little surprise,
but the other two, well they were tiny.
I could not believe my eyes!

It appeared as if they'd been playing.
Their tracks ran all over the lawn.
The big ones skirted the garden
up to the front door.......and were gone!

But the little steps turned in circles,
(and here was an odd thing to see)
they finally danced off together
to the trunk of the chestnut tree.

I followed this path on my tiptoes
and there on a toadstool of stone
smiling like imps at each other
sat my statuette leprechauns!

I really shouldn't have wondered,
I wouldn't have stood there in dread,
except that last weekend I'd stored them
for Winter in my garden shed!

The Blarney Stone

"For centuries the fairy folk have danced away the night,
'tis said if you were silent you might spy the wondrous
    sight
of little people whirlin' round to jigs and reels and all
and hear their magic music played on whistle and bodhran.
But even leprechauns get tired of endless merriment,
and often from the circle slip, their energy near spent,
to wander to a nearby glen, but never go alone,
to sit beneath the bright moonbeams upon the Kissin'
    Stone.
There many a fairy friendship bloomed into a fairy love
as arm in arm they'd talk 'till dawn crept o'er the hills
    above.
Then like the early morning mist they'd sort of float away
back to their secret kingdom hidden from the light of day."

"I know this story, Daddy, it's oft' told by you and Ma.
Still, how is it connected to yon' castle An Bhlarna?"

"Hould your whist, me buckoo, can't you see me pipe
    needs lit?
I'll fill the bowl, you get some turf and feed the fire a bit.
Now where was I? Oh, yes, the fairies' sacred place
just outside the village bounds where nothin' changed a
    trace
until one day a lord of means came to survey the land,
and seein' the glen announced that here his castle would
    soon stand.

He hired a hundred labourers, he paid for food and wine,
he made the villages prosperous, the castle grew in time.
In five short years it was complete, the money was all
    spent,
the lord invited all to join him on the battlements.
'Tis gran, 'tis truly grand,' they said. A smile spread on his
    face.
And then he frowned, and then he saw the gaping empty
    space.
'Where has the master builder gone? Bring him to me!' He
    cried.
'I'll have an explanation now or else I'll have his hide.'
'Alas the man has fled, me lord,' the foreman stammered
    on,
he couldn't do the job entire, the money bein' gone.'
'My castle won't be left like this! I'll be the laughing
    stock!'
The foreman's found his voice and said, 'I'll fix it with a
    rock,
a piece of limestone in the glen, 'tis known both far and
    near.'
'Take two men with you, hurry now, and bring the boulder
    here.'
A murmur rose among the host of neighbours gathered
    round.
They said, 'You can't touch that, me lord, it stands on fairy
    ground!
The wee folk will be vexed, me lord, when'er they find it
    gone.
They'll have revenge on him who dares to move their
    sacred stone.'

'This castle is my monument, an honour to my name.
I'll use the rock and by its use bestow eternal fame
on all the gentle fairy fold in Ireland's gentle land.
Their Kissin' Stone will be revered long as my home shall
stand.'
'How can this be?' Each asked in turn, each face indeed
perplexed.
'It's simple,' said the lord, 'whenever I shall have a guest
e'er he can take his leave from me he must fill my request
to lower himself, to show respect, to place a kindly kiss
upon the stone the wee folk gave to grant me final bliss.'"

The storyteller ends the tale and rising from his place
picks up the lad who's long asleep and softly strokes his
face.
"You've never heard this story through," he whispers with
a smile.
"Tomorrow night you'll beg again, 'Please Da, just one
more time.'
Your ancestors up there will dance a jig with fairy glee
to know I keep the promise that me father passed to me.
And I, to you in turn, me lad, will pass the honoured trust
of Blarney Castle's Kissin' Stone the fairies gave to us."

At Minus

The opiate of night lets slip its charm
and it were very bliss for me to yield
into the dreamy otherworldly realm
'rapt like a babe inside its mother's womb.

BRREEEEPP!!!

"Traffic and weather on the quarter hour."
That disquieting harbinger of day,
that unwelcome reliable surprise

was back again and wouldn't go away.
"The polar vortex dropping temperatures
across the region into values where

the likelihood of frostbite is severe.
Does not show any signs of moving on.
If you must venture out today be sure

to bundle up and that includes long johns.
At the airport it's minus twenty-eight.
The wind chill feels like minus forty-one."

The hum of warm air coming through the grate,
me beneath a dozen layers of down
and being retired decided I would wait

in bed until the Summer rolled around.
"Today the groundhog came out of his den
and when he saw his shadow on the ground

he did a turn about and went back in.
That's six more weeks of Winter, girls and boys
according to Willie's predictions."

Correcting how my blankets are deployed,
a stretch of limbs, a minor shift of core
draws in a draft that tickles my backside

soft as a clandestine lothario.
A little smile starts cheating 'cross my face;
we really must get out of bed, although...

At minus one the 'yeas' outweigh the 'nays.'
Snowfalls, snowballs, snowmen, snow angels bring
young and young-at-heart outside to play,

catching dancing snowflakes on the tongue
or walking hand-in-hand the blanching streets
beneath the languorous mid of Winter sun.

At minus fourteen Celsius degrees,
snow squeaks, birds flee, the sun seeks warmer climes.
A great white Northern layer of white concrete

entombs the land and even my behind
will feel its icy anaesthetic touch.
Not mischievous. Not subtle. Not sublime.

At minus twenty-eight hot water tossed
into the air evaporates. At night
ice quakes' deep voices boom below the crust.

Don't speak, just nod at any passerby
who knows your nose and his are frozen shut
and wasting breath on words is not advised.

But minus forty-one! That's cold enough
to freeze, you know, a monkey's pair of brass!
And water mains below the ground will burst

because it's colder than the planet Mars.
That's freaking cold! More cocoa darlin' then
climb back in here and warm my arse again.

The Dawn Chorus

A chilly draft of winter air
stirred the barn owl's fluffy down,
whistling in between the boards
on a slanting beam of light.

At first the owl was unaware
of the unfamiliar sound
coming from the space below
this brighter than expected night.

But having been asleep all day
he opened wide his small dark eyes
then bobbing his head back and forth
he looked and listened from his beam.

A mouse was moving in the hay...
but then he heard another noise,
a sound he hadn't heard before
and a sight he'd never seen.

He knew the shepherds came inside
whenever calves or lambs were born
but what the wooden manger held
was clearly not an animal.

It was instead a crying child
wrapped in cloth to keep him warm,
and his mother kissed his head,
and his father sang a song.

What happened next surprised the owl
who could only hiss or wheeze,
the sound of singing touched his heart
and he wished that he could too.

But he knew warblers who knew how
and larks and sparrows, chickadees,
robins, thrushes, even hawks,
and where they were, and off he flew.

It took a while, most of the night,
to round up such a flock of birds
of every colour shape and size
and lead them to his humble barn.

When they arrived before the light
they didn't peep nor chirp a word
but found a perch and turned their eyes
towards the east, towards the dawn.

Then as the sun announced the day
the song-less owl spread wide his wings
and all the birds began to sing
a chorus that was glorious,
glorious and continuous,
to glorify their new-born king
to pray as only birds can pray.

The Last Christmas Angel

Luke 2:9-15 In the countryside there are shepherds watching their flocks by night. The angel of the Lord appeared to them…..and suddenly with the angel there was a great throng of the heavenly host praising God and singing…..and when the angels had gone from them into heaven, the shepherds said to one another, "Let us go to Bethlehem to see this thing that has happened,"……….but

One angel lingered
just under the stars
watching the shepherds
securing the bars.
She said to herself
as they turned from their sheep,
"I'll stay close behind them
to get a wee peep."

So hovering she followed
them down to the shed
to come a bit closer
to Jesus' straw bed.
And when Joseph saw her
he gave her a nod
and pointed to Mary
and her infant God.

But as she descended
to stand on the ground
the tip of her wings
touched the nose of the cow.
She said, "Please excuse me,
I'm sorry for that,"
and nearly fell over
a drowsy old cat.

Not knowing the trappings
of men and their ways,
she stumbled around
on the straw and the hay.
When her foot found the end
of an overturned rake,
she muffled a cry
for the dear baby's sake.

She felt so embarrassed,
"I'm trying my best,"
when she tripped on the tail
of the donkey at rest.
The cow and the cat
and the donkey arose
to make room for the angel
to move, I suppose.

"Oh, dear, I believe
I have been here too long.
The morning draws near
and my choir has gone.
But I'm almost beside
Him in his little bed
and I'm ever so close
to His holy wee head."

Then she folded her wings,
put her hands into prayer,
and kissed Mary's baby
with heavenly care.
Her heart was so happy,
her soul sang with joy
as she paused in the doorway
to whisper goodbye.

The last Christmas angel
was soon out of sight
as the stars gave way
to the glimmering light.
And a little brown freckle
had bloomed on the cheek
where the angel had kissed
the wee babe in His sleep.

Original Sin

"Go on! Go on! Say it!
It's not so hard to do."

But she was silent,
her mouth would not be moved.
The word was violent!
It smacked of violence!
And yet she wanted to.

She watched her sister
bite on her bottom lip
then force her mouth into a cone
like an exploding volcano,
collapsing it abruptly upon
the final crowning consonant.
She listened to the sound;
the breath flying
forward, falling
into the lovely round vowel
that crashed at last
upon the brick.
It was beautiful!

"Go on! Go on! Say it!
It's not so hard to do."

Oh, she was tempted.
Her will was being wooed.
The word was violets.
It smelled of violets.
And yes! She wanted to!

Her sisters were bolder,
they'd broken other rules,
(one had become a smoker).
Still, she wouldn't call them vulgar.
They didn't use the word
in their daily speech.
They sat across from her
on the floor
of her darkened bedroom
waiting for her to say the word
that would make her
one of them.
It was dutiful!

"Go on! Go on! Say it!
It's not so hard to do!"

But she resisted.
She'd not become a fool.
The word was garbage!
It spawned in garbage!
She wouldn't go there too.

For her to yield,
for her to be untrue,
would leave within an emptiness
like the loss of a friend
who could never come back,
or be faithful as before.
Yet her sisters hadn't changed
from saying it,
had they?
They were still her friends,
would still be
no matter what she said,
wouldn't they?

"Go on! Go on! Say it!
It's not so hard to do!"

But she was silent.
Her mouth would not be moved.
The word was violent!
It smacked of violence!
And yet……she wanted to.

IRELAND

Stairs

On Skellig Michael
one rainy day in July
I saw her
tripping down the face

at suicidal speed,
her feet scarcely
touching the leading
edges of the holy

stepping stones
struck by monks
a thousand years
dead; a woodland

nymph on a treeless slide.
'Teens are good at this.
Sneakers or heels
become ballet slippers

at the top
of a set of steps,
dancing their feet
almost uncontrollably

to the bottom,
to walk away
unruffled by the flight.
I always watch

immobilized,
envious of their skill.
A student studied me
descending the altar

from the Lectern
at school Masses.
He said I led
with my heels,

and how uncool it looked.
My careful awkwardness
is a calculated risk.
Stairs call out to me

like sirens. From
summit to base
the journey's a desperate
descent on wobbly knees.

Climbing's a safer bet.
Years ago the terror
of hearing my child's
cry as he rolled down half

our seventeen wooden steps
tore me from sleep.
I prayed for both of us
thumping my way

heel by heel
to where he lay,
unruffled and unhurt.
I could have killed him.

All around the dangers
are disguised. Carpet
coverings, pebbled
foot grips, all weather

surfaces promise security.
Other promises
beckon from posters
along the way or grow

in polished pine planters,
massaging, assuring
the traveller
day by slippery day.

Like Diana's at Skelligs
flying with happy abandon,
it's a carefree
descent with a sudden stop.

I'd rather be upwardly mobile.
Give me Jacob's ladder any day!
It goes up only
and we can't see the top.

Came Upon

Burns_____ didn't give me his name
so I'll call him that_____,
was hunkered down on all fours
like a stalking cat,
face pressed against railings containing
the beaten path
on a wooded, secluded rise in St. Stephen's Green.

Good God! The man's insane!
A tailored suit
crawling on brambles and stones.
I turned to pursue
my way back into the light,
but he winked a salute
and shifted to manage a bit of space in between

bracken and ivy for me to enter
his shadowy world.
He returned his place at the bar,
said not a word,
then lifted his finger to point
where roots had curled
themselves a cantankerous knot like a braided nest,

barely perceptible given the layers
of tangle and shade.
Burns couldn't contain his frustration.
"Do you see them?" he said
as I started quaking and praying
for judgment day,
"Or are you just as woefully daft and blind as the rest?"

Then suddenly I saw them, thanks be to God!
A clutter of mice
poking and sniffing, exploring, retreating,
gone in a trice.
"There now," said Burns, proud as a peacock,
intense, erudite,
triumphantly brushing his coat, then back on his knees.

Here was a man more letter than litter,
more wondrous than odd,
mindful of courting his case reverential
on marble and sod.
Dismissing for better or worse the judgment
of tourists or God.
But how he came there in the first place still troubles me.

Standing on the Edge of the World

Here, from up here, St. Finan's Bay
is the last lap of the great North Atlantic Sea.
Grey as grief, Kerry blue blazers swept away
by another ominous armada
of Nimbostratus invading the bay.
The waters lie in wait. On the edge

of the world, Ciarán and I brace ourselves
for the wallop of wind, sudden drench
of rain and night soon to be realized
in breathtaking huzzah astonishment.
His sensible mother and sister
sit in the car and wait in dread suspense.
Maybe the two of us will disappear
when the wall arrives. "Bloody fools.
They could have watched it from in here
and stayed dry."
                    But the tableau is hypnotic.
Our summer jackets not meant
for this kind of weather are zipped
to the chin. Hard clenched fists stretch
our pockets as we stand transfixed
and I more than a little unnerved.

Behind us hump and hollow hills
idly embrace the sea,
soft sloped shoulders sliding
with casual ease
into the waves. From the West
the stalking front of shameless duplicity.

I shift to contact my
son who smiles a smile that says
he understands and I am braver
and pleased I did not overplay
the act. I must have closed my eyes
then and missed the cannonade.

I never felt a thing until the whole world
closed in like a hostile shroud,
leaving me disabled, listening and straining
for anything familiar, light or sound.
But we were standing in a drizzle
of nothingness, on insecure ground

trying to secure foothold of confidence.
Ciarán nudged me out of my dream
and said, "This way to the car."
                              I went
where he pointed, the sodden air

parting before and closing behind our diffident
forms. Somewhere along the way
He stopped and turned to face the sea.
Submerged in the phantom abyss
he threw up his arms in triumph; "Wasn't that great?!"

Clare Island

When I heard her say almost aloud,
"God, I'd love to know what's in that box!"
Pleasure and surprise
misshaped my face.

How did I miss it earlier that day?
I think now the ghost of Granuaile
and Clare Island's skies
got in the way.

No matter where we went along the quay
acrid diesel fumes were all we got,
that and near the gangplank's
shifting rail

a clump of hikers eager to depart
to Louisburgh for fish and chips and stout.
I too was glad to find
an empty seat.

Clare Island! Summer roost for Granuaile,
pirate queen of Ireland nonpareil
who'd met another queen
in London town

to plead her case and come away unscathed.
Once upon a time it was my quest
to find her kin
and look into her face

for traces of the hardness of the sea.
But all I found was such a lovely girl
as innocent and timid
as a breeze.

Her father's stature spoke O'Malley lines
but he too was a man of honest means.
Not what I expected.
Or desired.

A scribbled note tacked beside the lock
on Rockfleet's heavy door collided with
my 'New World' sensibility
and trust.

"Go to the farmhouse for the key." Full stop!
I told myself these Irish must be mad!
A tattered note!
Call that security?

Call it guilt or conscience if you will,
the thought that hounded me along the lane,
I'd said '*these*' Irish
and the bitter pill

of persona non grata hit me hard.
As I write this now I feel the sting
of living here
where not my heart belongs.

Another note; "The key is underneath
the saucer on the window sill." Why not!
Throw history open
to the passing horde!

Their car arrived before I turned away,
immobilized me like a bumbling thief.
I almost put my
hands behind my back.

That clever little schemer Graine Mhaile
had cut her hair to join her father's crew.
Had undermined his wrath
with snip and pluck.

A half a thousand years like a cold draft
sweeping underneath a distant door
across the yard
as if nothing had changed,

seemed to me as close as yesterday.
What man is there who never turned to mush
as I like he,
was utterly destroyed

by sloe-brown eyes? "Hello," she said and then
"Don't forget to put it back before
you leave." She took her father's hand
and smiled.

I trudged the upward grade between the hills
that roughly part the island East and West
from where the sea
cannot be seen or heard.

My wife and her companions trailed behind.
They might as well have been a hundred years
beyond my solitude
and reverie.

To get close to the question, step by step
wretchedness encountered, door and dune,
wind and sea and words
and East and West,

I kept my head down. There might have been
wet ditches, skittish sheep, sudden gorse
shepherding my way
like native guides,

I don't remember anything of these.
But '*these*' Irish things tormented every step.
Threatened consequences.
Lay in wait.

I wish it could be tied into a knot,
wrapped and labelled, 'Soon to be forgot,'
put into the lunchbox
crushed and tucked

underneath my arm. A few more strides
and the Western sea spread out likc glass
bright and fragile,
silent as the sky.

I was still standing there head upright
when caught off guard by sudden cool updraft
of strange perfume,
dry seaweed, sea-wet wood.

A perfect day for pirating! Stout breeze,
Clear skies. Swift ship. A merchantman beyond.
Granuaile of steely eyes
and cold,

disarming one more unsuspecting mark.
Let it be said of me when I am known,
a paradigm of lost
between two worlds,

I own some grains of salty sea and stone
more Celt than concrete, gushing through my veins
to which I give assent
this Island day.

The ferry's underway. Spent passengers
slouch or doze. But I can hear her mind
scheming. Dying to unlid
my empty box.

S.H.

They call it The Bucket List.
Things you want to do, places
you want to go before you go.
Mine, 'though never writ nor spoken,
was short. One entry, to be exact,
and now I have to call it back
because the man I wanted to meet
is dead.

To be sure, I walked his Irish streets.
The chaff blown corn fields where
he planted words, the linear
potato drills, bogs of turf,
tinkers camping beside a lough,
these places and things that shaped me
too, this thread is broken now for
he is dead.

Words, never few nor spare,
never restrained, seemed to pour
from his pen, the conduit weapon
for everything came upon.
His was a holy and wholly lived
life because of that gift.
But I, I am somehow lesser because
he is dead.

In my most secretive thoughts
I imagined a few pints of stout,
an afternoon of good craic,
his patient expansive Socratic
questions and observations,
my Plato-like hanging on
to every word. Forever lost.
He is dead.

Consonant exploiter.
Voluminous voweller.
Champion of commonplace.
Bard of the Irish race.
Singer of lovers' songs.
Righter of troubled wrongs.
You who have sanctified
those who are cast aside,
opened the heart
with your sonorous breath.
Bereft at your leaving,
I scribble this grieving
at the most sorrowful
news of your death.

Play Me A Reel

Play me a reel.
Play me a reel that I might dance
a dance lively bowed
on a fiddle with
merry whistling alongside
and a bodhran to keep time.

Play me a reel,
a toe-tapping set of reels
that neither end or begin
but slide from one to another
seamless like sunlit water
over round stones
in a brook.

Play me a reel
that's not been heard for years.
A reel that stops me still
to ponder the last time
I heard the tune or saw
it danced.

Play me a reel,
a reel that stirs my heart
to brew there a tiny drop
of ancient happiness
sending it spiralling onward
along a silken chord
to well in my eyes.

Play me a reel,
a sweet singing song of a reel
flying from life giving gratitude
into the soul of God's creature
blest by its spell.

Play me a reel.
Play it and never stop playing
that I might be caught in the mystery
that binds me over and over
to the call of my homeland,
that mystical land
of Eirne.

The Weaver of Stone

There is in the west, an eternal supply
of un-quarried limestone,
chunks and slabs and slivers,
broken, unbroken, bits of dry
purposeless stone, the sweepings
of heaven at the end of creation
scabbing the scant soil.

Or it might be Cain's legacy
cast on the Irish race
for their sins, cursing Connaught
and the cold dark-island
dwellers to lifelong labour and pain,
bending and lifting and pitting
their backs against the pitiless stone.

Above this wretched landscape
hangs the great grey sky.
A wollen blanket reservoir
of rain, cold and constant
as the ground it scours
where neither forest nor garden
finds depth of hold.

A thousand years of practice—
some experts say thirty hundred years—
our ancestors learned and taught.
These men of the west, sharp-eyed surveyor,
engineer, geologist, excavator,
archeologist, geographer, balancer,
leveller, geometer, labourer,

Architect, artist, puzzle-solver,
land-bound navigator, astronomer,
each in his own time a master
builder, the never-ending lattice
of stone walls, his masterpiece.
He is building eternity,
he, the poetic weaver of stone.

You'll not find bond nor mortar
securing the walls. He reads
the line, the shape, the grain
of each stone, feels its weight,
its centre of gravity, tests it
against its neighbour then
shifts the piece into place. Precisely.

The wall holds against itself.
The waist height is consistent. It buffers
the sweeping scythe of North Atlantic wind
protecting the short grass for grazing.
Each parcel of field is defined
by the walls. Each wall is defined
by the weaver's hand.

Here, the uppermost layer rests
on a double base; stones braced
on the vertical or horizontal plane
almost impervious to light,
so carefully are they placed.
There, the order seems disordered
yet the stones stand, time-defiant.

Stone gates are imposed into the walls
like accidental inverted pyramids
easily removed for passage, easily
restored without compromising the weave
of the whole. Look. Some genius eye
left spaces for the rising sun
to shape the shade of Mary onto the grass.

The weaver of stone knows no reward.
Glory is never his desire.
His opus cannot be framed.
All we can do is shake our head
in reverential fear failing
to comprehend. Walk alongside the walls
which lead and lead and lead.

Inis Oirr

You can tell me again and again,
and I will believe again
that the island is there,
that the boat is taking us there
and that we will arrive.
                    Aahh!
All I can do is sigh,
know the grey descending sky
and try to imagine a shape
into being for my own sake,
reminding me I am alive.
                    Far
ahead, beyond my sight
through the grey-on-grey non-light
in the mist, lies Inis Oirr,
waiting and waiting for me.
                    When
did we leave the pier and how?
I don't remember it now
'though the lullaby lapping of waves
and the way the boat behaves
tells me we are at sea.
                    Nothing
remains to define;
no familiar dimensions, not even time.
Behind us lies what was sure.
Out here the enchanted lure
of Tir na N'Og and the West.

LIMITATIONS

Penance

I can't say where Belmont Avenue begins or ends but when we needed some groceries, I picked it up three traffic lights and a few more streets from the apartment to the store. I was buying asparagus, bananas, carrots, cheese chicken and milk in alphabetical order so as to calculate the running costs not to be caught short of cash at the checkout.

It was during this process that a young grey-eyed packer, my re-usable grocery bag in her hand, asked me whether she should put the milk in. I suggested she carry the milk bag to the apartment for me instead, trying to evoke a smile. She failed to grasp the humour and immediately went to another counter to talk to a co-worker about whether the colour of nail polish should match the colour of eyes.

I finished packing myself and store exited turned into the wind to retrace the twenty minute walk which I feared would be more onerous due to the weight of the foodstuffs now helping the bag handles bite into my fingers with every burdensome step. By the time I was approaching the first traffic light, red in my direction necessitating a welcome stop-and-wait interruption, the bag had been switched from one hand to the other to restore circulation in my fingers. I wasn't looking forward to the rest of this journey.

It was a sunny afternoon, about nine degrees Celsius I should think, so I had the need to unzip my coat as my core body temperature was rising from the strain of the journey and my heart was working harder to accommodate aching limbs and effort. The coolness of the breeze provided some relief even if it was purely psychological.

There was a woman a few steps in front of me who had paused to await the green light. At the opposite corner the red hand flashed, decades dissolved and I was walking to school, a carefully calculated distance behind the Loretto High School co-ed whose plain black shift

329

accented only by white plastic collar and cuffs made her look a miniature nun like the Sisters who taught us. She had tied around her waist a narrow scarf that pulled her dress slightly above her knees, accentuating her young womanly figure which swayed every so slightly and provocatively as she walked. I with my blazer open, tie askew, paced my steps to insure I could never catch up to the object of my tempered Catholic desire less she turn around and I would have to gaze with stupidity into her undoubtedly gorgeous eyes. I told myself that with my own eyes I was committing at least two capital sins five days a week. When we arrived at the school steps, off came her sash and I fixed my tie and blazer. She mounted the left steps, I took the right side. Oddly enough, we never saw each other the rest of the day.

Today the woman crossed before I did but her pace suggested she was not trying to get well ahead in case I might be someone to be feared or at the very least an unsavoury character. In her left hand was one of those retractable dog leash devices whose cord allowed an investigative loaf-of-bread sized grey poodle to remain under her control. The dog's owner was about five foot eight, of slim but not slender build, wearing fashionable form fitting blue jeans, a light blue sweater and above it a voluminous stack of blonde hair secured by a gossamer white bandana.

I decided she was probably in her mid thirties. Just as she gained the other side of the street, the dog darted behind her necessitating the woman perform a pirouette to untangle the leash. I switched my bag from left to right hand in a gesture of solidarity and catching a glimpse of her sun-glassed face was surprised to discover I was perhaps twenty years short in guessing her age. Her action and my pace brought us side by side so I offered, "Nice day, isn't it?"

(Later in retrospect, I regretted using the word "nice" to describe what was in fact a glorious or beautiful or spectacular Spring afternoon, anything but "nice.")

Her long narrow face accentuated by high cheek bones and an angular nose was not unattractive. Her hair was dyed blonde with patches of grey beginning to show through. I thought she might be a little sad.

The dog moved across our path to sniff a lamp post. I returned the weighty bag to my left hand establishing a sort of wall between our two bodies to allay any fears she might take from my proximity.

She replied, "Yes, it is a wonderful day," a more magnanimous assessment than the "nice" I had assigned. I noticed a slight accent and took a chance.

"You're Polish?"

"Yes, I am."

"How long have you been here?"

"My son who is nineteen was born shortly after we arrived."

By offering this detail she was actually telling me she was married, had a family so don't get any ideas.

"I have a son-in-law who is Polish and married to one of my four daughters."

By this I meant that I too was married, have a family and therefore need not be feared. My four queens trumped her ace and she could not know I had three kings to play should that become necessary.

"Where are you from?" she enquired obviously having detected my own accent as Europeans often do. At this point my fingers were becoming numb so the bag was passed into my right hand.

"I'm Irish."

"Oh, are you from Dublin?"

"No. I'm from the Midlands where the tourists never go."

"But you have wonderful milk and cheese," she said, almost in compensation for my uninteresting demographics.

We fell into an amiable stride a little more relaxed with each other's company, she doing most of the talking.

And so it went on for two more traffic lights where she turned into a side street, the dog peed on a flowering shrub and once again the bag was transferred right to left, or was it left to right? But it was during those final blocks of our walk that I learned about her city of birth, her views of Canadians and their obvious fragility should an act of terrorism like a suicide bomber ever happen here, her disdain for Europe's open borders and its secular Godlessness. She talked about her pride of being Polish because the Poles always overcome adversity and threw in a few other opinions she thought I wanted to hear including the pleasure she finds in meeting new people and that my eyes are blue and piercing.

She was a talker given the chance and maybe hadn't been very often so I had become a willing listener.

The apartment building came into my view and I thanked God I wouldn't have to carry the weight much further. I looked behind me but the streets were empty.

The Polish woman was gone.

"*Piercing*" blue eyes, I thought. "Hhmmh."

Sadly, I cannot tell you the colour of her eyes.

Contrition

Lillian started clenching and grinding her teeth a few minutes after entering the church. She had arrived half-an-hour early for the Healing Mass and parked her wheelchair half way up the wide side aisle. That's when she became anxious.

Her unobstructed view of the altar revealed a plain unadorned table about six feet long and three feet wide. Behind it centred against an equally featureless wooden wall were three ordinary chairs, one for the priest the others for servers. A fourth chair was out of place in front of the altar. She could not find the Tabernacle nor a side repository where it might be reserved.

This was the reason for her anxiety, the absence of holy objects in a new Catholic church which didn't have any of the trappings one might expect to find in any

Christian edifice. The pews were designed not to hold hymnals or prayer books. The windows were tall narrow clear glass affairs, the Stations of the Cross small clay tiles in colourless relief. Nowhere could she find candles or statues or a crucifix. And no one would have noticed her lips move as she muttered a curse upon the architect and the hour she had spent dangerously secured in the van travelling to this obviously God-forsaken place.

Lillian's wheelchair was new too, the third one she had owned and easiest to operate from the joystick on the right arm rest. Even with her severely misshapen arthritic hand, she could manoeuvre the chair with great subtlety in any direction.

Behind her shoulders her back was slightly hunched, her feet become club-like, her hands unable to grasp due to awkward angular appendages that used to be fingers. She had come to be healed by the foreign priest who was said to have a gift and was making the rounds. She didn't expect her body to be made whole, just to find relief from the pain and to pray that Paddy would find his Catholic faith once again.

Lillian's friends were sitting in the pew beside her. From time to time one of them would look towards her and smile but she was unaware. She let her head fall back on the headrest and closed her eyes. When she opened them, there was a man kneeling before her.

Life had not been kind since she arrived in Canada almost forty years earlier, four young children in tow, chasing after a husband who had come eighteen months in advance to secure work and a place to live. Within ten years their marriage was over, her health was deteriorating and she had to rely on social assistance for her family to survive. And those ten years had been a tumultuous riot of sex, alcohol and violence perpetuated by the party crowd who revered Paddy for his startling good looks and RAF war stories. Booze and bawdy songs kept the wife-swapping weekends alive starring Eric the big red, Paddy the tail gunner, Jean the machine and 'what's mine's yours' Winnie. Frequently somebody got out of line and insults, threats and punches were thrown. Rent money was gone by Monday morning and in a few months they were thrown out, a cycle which repeated itself annually that desperate decade.

The very day Paddy left, he had come home drunk, thrown a plate of dinner across the kitchen and tried to strangle Lillian who broke free and locked herself in the bathroom. They never saw each other again until the wedding day of their eldest son and Paddy demonstrated a little sensibility by not bring his new wife with him.

Abandoning the family had not given him the freedom he said he wanted to have. For one thing, his party buddies didn't support his decision and eventually the good times came to an end. Nor could he hold a job for any length of time. Always looking for a uniform he had become a police officer but was dismissed for accepting bribes from speeding motorists. Then he was a prison guard for some years during which he passed cigarettes and other favours to the inmates and was caught. Next job as a security guard was short lived. There was talk of stolen goods on his shift and he was let go but that was of little consequence because he was carrying on with a woman who had some money and was willing to marry and support him.

They bought a camper and spent the summer months rambling around the country, meeting other free spirits, drinking, singing, screwing which is what he was doing when the first heart attack cut him short. The day he was released from the hospital he told the nurses he had some "unfinished business" to attend and they laughed at his wickedness and swooned at his striking good looks. After that he and his wife seemed to have vanished and neither Lillian nor the family heard any rumours or stories about him for years.

The Healing Priest waited for the usher's signal then took his place on the forward chair. The church went dead quiet and in a calm assuring voice he explained how the process would go. Starting from the back people would be escorted in groups of six to stand beside him, three on each side, hands resting on his outstretched arms. He would recite the healing prayers and a blessing then invite the next six to come up. There would be helpers standing around his chair to support or catch anyone who might stumble or fall.

This went on for more than an hour and all the time Lillian kept her eyes closed in restful prayer. Her friends would guide her wheelchair forward when their group was called. They knew she should not be disturbed until that time.

As the sick and the saddened, the weary, the worried, those crippled of body and spirit shuffled to and from the priest, the low sound of singing voices underpinned by soft organ music wafted over the saints and sinners like musical incense making the very air holy and healing. An intoxicating balm of Latin phrases and soothing heavy air poured over Lillian like a sonorous liquid blanket penetrating her senses and pores. She felt her body become weightless, her pains sliding away, her feather-light soul surrendering, surrendering when the weight of a hand touched her forearm.

Slightly startled and annoyed at the interruption to the ecstasy she blinked her eyes open and lifted her head. It took what seemed an eternity to accommodate to her surroundings, the forms and faces around and near to her but when she did, she gasped audibly before becoming utterly speechless.

It was Paddy, her Paddy, down on both knees, one hand holding the end of the pew, the other on her arm.

She couldn't guess how long he'd been there or how he had found her but when he moved upward and closer she didn't feel the need to pull away. He hovered a moment then grasping the pew, pulled himself up to his feet and left. One of Lillian's friends asked if she was okay, and did she need any help and had that man spoken to her or threatened her. Lillian didn't respond immediately but when she did she told her friend the only thing she was willing to reveal, that the man had uttered three words and three words only in her ear and that those three words were, "Please forgive me."

Intimidation

At Colin's thirteenth birthday party, his father put a loaded .45 calibre pistol into Robby's hands and told him to point at the tree.

Robby was the same age as Colin and went to the same school but they could hardly be called friends. Their relationship pivoted around Colin's pretty blonde girlfriend Vickie who held a secret crush on Robby and had invited him to Colin's for the party. Her parents had driven them to the farm and would bring them home after dinner. Colin's father had motioned the three of them away from the music and dancing and they were standing behind the barn when he produced the gun.

"Hold it with both hands.

Stretch your arms out in front of you like this.

Use your eye to aim along the barrel at the tree trunk.

Take a deep breath.

Exhale.

Stay still.

Now, squeeze the tri__"

BANG!

The suddenness of the explosion, his hands recoiling wildly shocked Robby wide-eyed.
"Holy shit!"

"You have to squeeze the trigger gently, not jerk it!" Colin's father said.

"No thanks. That's too scary. You can have it back."

Colin was laughing himself silly as his friends came running to see what happened but his father was already taking the gun back inside.

"You're such a dork, afraid of a gun."

"Leave him alone," said Vickie. "I don't like guns either."

Robby said nothing more. He could still feel in his hands the tingling from the shot, the ringing in his ears might never go away. He decided he would never shoot a gun again. Real guns are not toys. Somebody could get hurt.

After that Colin gave him more attention at school. They ate lunch together, walked the halls together and sought each other's company between classes. By summer they were buddies.

One weekend in August Colin's parents were going to the city but he wasn't interested and Robby was invited to sleep over. Country folk watch what is going on around them and with no car in the driveway, the house became a target for a break-in. Colin was awakened by unfamiliar noises in the yard and quickly alerted Robby. They heard attempts to force open the kitchen door.

Colin placed two chairs together, told Robby to sit down then opened a closet. He handed him the pistol and took out a shotgun for himself.

"Undo the safety," he whispered, "and point at the bottom of the door. We'll blow their fucking knees off."

Voices indicated there were at least two intruders using their shoulders and feet to force the door but it was made of solid wood and wouldn't budge. Eventually they gave up and drove away much to Robby's relief and Colin's disappointment. Their parents were never told about the incident.

It is an oddity in life that sometimes the thing you want most to avoid has a way of coming after you and so it happened about four years later they joined the local militia and as required, went one day to the firing range for training. On his own Robby would have never entered the armed forces but reluctantly he went along with Colin who would not have let him live it down if he refused. Besides, the money was good and it was a part time job that would be over in two years.

Their weapon was the Belgian made UN issue FN rifle capable of killing a man at a kilometre. It recoiled up instead of backwards and had to be tucked securely between shoulder and cheek for best control. They fired a five-round clip from a prone position at targets 200 metres away. Robby sighted his target and pulled the trigger. The butt jumped into his cheek, rattling every bone in his head.

"That's enough for me," he mumbled and started to rise but the sergeant placed his left boot on his backside and shoved him down.

"Finish two clips then I'll let you up."

And Robby did as ordered. He held the trigger back firing four rounds in less than a second, changed the clip and did the same again. Then he stood at his post and waited for the others to finish.

The sergeant wasn't impressed. "You have to learn not to be afraid of guns. Come with me."

They mounted a jeep and drove to the concrete trench where the targets were raised and lowered.

"Get down there soldier and run up a target."

Robby scrolled the chain, the target went up over his head and a few seconds later shots were fired. The shooter was wild and soon dirt and debris were flying everywhere, the target's metal frame was struck by a bullet and Robby feared for his safety. He hated guns.

The following year they were trained to operate 105mm howitzers, the field artillery used to lob shells at distant targets. At the practice range he was assigned to pull the lanyard, the last of five steps required to shoot the weapon. He was happy that a howitzer was less 'personal' than a pistol or rifle and his job was carried out with his back to the gun. In a few hours his team had shown notable efficiency with blank ammunition and were promptly given ten live rounds. The first shell was loaded, the command given to 'fire' and Robby obeyed.

BOOM! went the gun, the breach quickly opened, spent casing ejected, a new round inserted and the command to 'fire' was called again.

BOOM!

Eight more times the gun roared and the exercise was completed. For Robby it hadn't come fast enough and he was more relieved when his stint as a soldier finally ended. Maybe now he could rest assured that his encounter with guns was over at last and forever.

That was many years ago and he has neither been close to or seen a gun since except in media reports on fanatics and terrorists using bombs and guns to destabilize regions or make travel unsafe. As a tourist he is aware of heightened security at airports, train and bus stations. He has encountered armed soldiers strolling around these places unnerving and reassuring him at the same time. He accepts that such steps have to be taken and tries not to think about the risks.

But guns continue to haunt him and invade his personal space even in the least likely circumstances.

Among his most beloved friends is a family with five children all under the age of ten and as innocent of the world as newborn lambs in Spring. Robby admires the attractive common sense mother and tells himself he might even be in love with her if he wasn't twice her age. They live in a house with a big backyard where climbing trees overlook the gardens planted as projects in their homeschool curriculum. Told stories and books come before television, music lessons and museum visits dot their calendar and the youngest raises a mess in the kitchen helping to make chocolate chip cookies. Sunday church and goodnight prayers are lifestyle as are visits from family and friends.

Seven other young children inhabit the homes on either side and the three yards are unfenced playground for the lambkins, happy and innocent, best buddies all. It is an idyllic life for children, so Robby thinks.

He was standing on the deck with his friends Lena and Peter last week when Peter mentioned his deep concern for the future of the kiddies playing beyond. Lena turned to her husband, "I think we're prepared for any eventuality, don't you Peter?"

She gave Robby a friendly pat on his shoulder and went into the house.

When she returned she walked straight up to him and thrust into his hands a semi-automatic Russian assault rifle.

"That should keep the bad guys away," she chirped.

Lollygaggers

The last meeting In Defence of Lollygaggers Everywhere was scheduled for June 21 but had to be postponed for lack of a quorum. Someone, who-knows-who, was supposed to read minutes from the previous gathering but nobody ever wanted to take notes so that might not happen and maybe everyone didn't check their email so who knows who would show up this last Sunday in June.

The venue was Joe's second storey deck some 20 feet above ground level among Aspen, Oak and Hemlock trees whose branches reached out towards the railings. Here were six cushioned easy care chairs, a weathered teak table and a barbecue. The last Sunday in June was a day of blue skies, warm sunshine and a delightful little breeze that turned the Aspen leaves into dancing droplets of greenery. Through the sliding screen door into the kitchen a cooler of beer and white wine stood on a chair near the table where there were a few bottles of red, several bagged snacks, a cheese plate and a bowl of salad. Those attending were expected to have earlier consumed a hearty lunch to stave off hunger and encourage a warm afternoon lethargy. The barbecue's cover was not coming off this day.

Joe was pleased with his preparations or rather his wife's who was not a member and didn't want to be thought of as an unwelcoming host. She wouldn't hang around when the others arrived. Yes, Joe was a happy man sprawling in his favourite chair under the summer sun, made happier when his wife brought him a cold one just as the door bell rang.

"I'll get it," she said, "Then be off on my 10k."

Mandy showed herself at the screen. Joe said, "Help yourself."

"Thanks, Joe. I will. Am I the first one here?"

"Yup."

Mandy had turned forty this year and like Joe's wife, had not given birth to any children so her body was still curvy and desirable. She was wearing a yellow tee shirt, slightly too big, Joe thought, and pyjama-loose blue slacks. When she emerged through to the deck, she was barefoot and had slid her sunglasses through her long auburn hair like a hairband. Mandy never put makeup on her glowing complexion. She looked twenty-something years old and moved without haste, not ever in a hurry to get anywhere.

"Sit over there," Joe pointed.

As she flopped into the chair, Joe had ideas. His wife was out and he and Mandy were alone. He always had ideas about Mandy but couldn't be bothered. She took a sip of her wine. Most of the time she drank red but today it was white. "Are all the others coming?" She looked into the trees with indifference avoiding Joe's attention. She knew Joe wanted to get his hands on her and if he didn't have that gut and receding hairline, she might have encouraged him. They were about the same age but Joe looked his and she thought he would be very slow and deliberate, much suited to her own pace of life. "I was going to bring some dessert but left it too late."

They didn't speak for the next ten minutes but it was not an awkward silence. Once, Joe put his head back and yawned and Mandy smiled weakly at him. Apart from that they were inert until a voice called out, "Anybody home?"

"Out here," Joe shouted. Take something on the way through."

"Hey Cindy, JP," said Mandy. "Grab a seat."

Each of them had a beer and JP was carrying a bowl of cheesies so he pulled a chair across with his foot. He was wearing cut-off shorts and flip-flops and a polo shirt with food stains down the front. Cindy wore a floral summer dress. Joe looked her up and down. She was not his type, a little plump and too chatty for his liking.

"I was saying to JP coming over here I couldn't remember if anyone took notes last time. I don't remember seeing anyone writing. I brought a note pad in case. I got this dress from my mother. Do you like it? Can't be bothered shopping for clothes these days. Quit my job last week. Didn't like the hours. Besides JP makes enough with his programming or something job. He'll be working from home starting next month, won't you sweetie? That way I can sleep in."

"You guys out on the deck?" The brothers Lentement, Guy and Alain had arrived. "C'mon through and get something for yourselves," Joe replied, relieved that Cindy's boring monologue had been cut off.

"We were going to take in nine holes, but, you know, nice day, don't want to waste it chasing a ball around," Guy said. Alain nodded in agreement and sat down. Each wore dark tops and blue slacks but there the similarities ended, Guy being a shapeless 200 pound, six foot tall man, Alain more like a fit Sumo wrestler, about the same weight as his brother but some four inches shorter.

JP tipped his class towards Joe. "Thanks for organizing the meeting. It's been a while. Cindy can take notes when we get on with the business. Who took minutes last time?" He waited for an answer but it wasn't coming. Joe noticed Mandy had finished her drink. "Can I get you another one of those Mandy? Hey JP fetch Mandy the Chardonnay and bring some more of those snacks out here too."

When he came back he was carrying a tray with several bottles of beer and wine and bowls of chips and cheesies. "You guys can take care of yourselves," he mumbled.

Under the persistent sun and cloudless blue sky combined with alcohol consumed, the group, sprawled in their chairs, eyes closed or partially closed, settled into a period of silence that stretched into the afternoon. It was Cindy who broke the reverie by rising cautiously and ask in an almost apologetic voice, "Did we have an agenda today?" Bodies began to squirm and shift, Cindy fidgeted with her fingers, Joe sneered at her and was about to speak when Mandy shocked him. "I was wondering that too." She went over to Cindy and said something inaudible to her. The two women embraced then linked arms, and surveyed the group, inviting a reply.

Guy took a deep breath and cleared his throat. "I think I dozed off," he said looking towards his brother. "But the girls are right. What are the plans, guys?" Alain nodded. Joe and JP said nothing.

"Who took notes last time?" It was Mandy again, her voice had a slight edge that demanded a proper answer this time.

Cindy sat down, fetched her purse from under the chair and extricated a steno pad and pencil. "I'll take the minutes."

Joe could see that unless he took charge, things could get out of hand or worse, the group might become too serious and business-like. "I made some notes," he lied, "But I don't remember where I put them. As this is our last meeting before the Fall, let's agree to plan for a whole year when we get back together in September."

Cindy recorded every word.

The four men looked at each other in agreement.

Mandy flopped back into her chair. "Is there any white wine left?"

Casualties

A few days after his eighteenth birthday they told Doc he had murdered me. The facts were clear, the evidence more than circumstantial. I was dead and had been made dead by Doc, Friday afternoon behind the gymnasium.

The truth is I had spent a few hours in the hospital late Friday afternoon but had gone home under my own steam as well as could be given the circumstances. But few people knew that. By Monday the story of my murder was buzzing through the school hallways and cafeteria with Doc's name at the centre. The truth is I wasn't in school that day or the rest of the week because of the concussion and pounding headache and the truth is I was still alive.

But the Cool Guys told Doc he had killed me.

Every school has its generations of Cool Guys and Hot Girls; the guys with attitude and influence and entitlement who hung around in groups in the hallways or on the corners of school property smoking, judging, intimidating; the girls who are acutely aware of their beauty or imagined beauty, for whom everyone moves aside when they approach, about whom the cool guys are vulgar and the rest of the world, male and female, can only dream about having or being.

These Cool Guys told Doc he had killed me. The Hot Girls turned heel when they saw him, a murderer in their school.

But because these circles were closed and one of the Cool Guys had been there and witnessed the event, details about my death were never going to be available to the less privileged and Doc being one, couldn't ask questions or seek information. The accused was to be told nothing except I was dead at his hands and my absence from school was proof enough.

Doc didn't come to school Tuesday. The Hot Girls hardly noticed but the Cool Guys did and they began to worry. One of them, The Witness, became the centre of their suspicions. What did you *really* see? How did it *actually* happen? What did *you* do?

The Witness noticed a change in attitude. The whispers were about him now and he found himself alone between classes and everyone seemed to have vanished from their preferred meeting places. He found himself always one step behind, arriving just as they were leaving or turning the corner ahead of him at the other end of the hall or skipping classes without inviting him. He thought everyone in the school was looking at him, judging him, knowing all that he knew and even more. He felt sick to his stomach and the horrible possibility that I might be dead after all planted itself in his fears. He found a bathroom cubicle and locked himself in.

The Witness had reason to be terrified but not so terrified as was Doc still lying in his bed going over the events trying to separate fact from fiction. Doc's efforts to relive the incident was proving almost impossible because aside from his anxiety, Doc is legally blind. Whatever happened that day was more a blur than a sharp recall but he does remember the struggle and my sudden cry and The Witness running back into the school leaving him standing over my body with a shovel in his hands.

Dominic Bartelli had earned the nickname "Doc" because of his astounding memory which was now, ironically, failing him. From about the Fourth Grade he had wowed everyone with his remarkable ability to recall a conversation exactly as it had unfolded. He remembered everything he was told or taught or heard on the radio, television or movies. He knew what was happening around his neighbourhood and the world. Details recall was especially strong and he was accommodated at exam time by being permitted to sit them orally while everyone else was writing.

Dominic Bartelli was a candidate for the coveted School Letter Award in this his graduating year and rumours had him favoured as valedictorian. True, the choice was not without a modicum of sentimentality. His sight had been deteriorating again but his spirit wasn't flagging.   He had won admiration and sympathy from students and staff and his send off was going to be memorable, more to him than anyone else in the whole world.

Tuesday afternoon, still in bed, Dominic Bartelli didn't give a damn for school letters and speeches. Dominic Bartelli was a young man without a plan. I was dead, murdered in fact and he didn't know how to shake himself from his paralysis.

At the same time Doc was suffering his private hell, I was comfortably pillowed on a sofa watching afternoon game shows on television, cursing an annoying headache, the only evidence that apart from a few stitches in my scalp that I had been struck on the head by a shovel.

Last period last Friday Doc, The Witness and I were excused from gym class to refresh the long jump pit prior to the upcoming Field Day.   The Witness appointed himself field marshall, gave me the rake, Doc the shovel and he did the measuring.   Doc began to loosen the compacted sand with me at his heels raking the turn over into a level surface.   Apparently we were too slow for The Witness who decided to do the digging himself but Doc would not be talked out of his job and when The Witness tried to wrench the shovel from his grip, they stood in the middle of the pit flailing the tool around like an out of control one-armed windmill and my head got in the way. When The Witness reported to the office a teacher arrived, took me to the hospital and Doc went home.

About the same time I was easing myself to my feet to change the channel, I heard a knock on the door, not a confident knocking but a tentative tapping as if its instigator didn't want it to be answered.   I waited a minute and it came again, three spaced taps a little louder than the first round.   One hand on the wall, I approached the door slowly and opened it enough to see who was there.   At first he said nothing, just stood there squinting but when I drew the door back fully Dominic Bartelli threw his arms around my shoulder and started to cry.   He held me like that a long time, until his sobbing subsided then he pulled back and looked into my eyes.

It all came out in a torrent of surprise, relief, an apology, his horrible weekend, the stories of my death, his guilt and shame, his decision to explain to my parents, but most of all, now that I was alive, what could he do to help me feel better. I invited him in and we talked some more but we never mentioned The Witness.

Doc won his school letter but one of the Hot Girls gave the valedictory address.

About three years later I read a news article about Dominic Bartelli who was struck by a car while crossing a street in a far away city. He was pronounced dead at the scene.

Mary

Mary Kelly lives alone. She has lived alone in the middle unit of a row of drab townhouses for more than 30 years. She bought it outright when she was 45 years of age with money she won from a lottery. Mary keeps her house tidy and warm as if she might expect visitors to knock on her door at any moment. Possession is not something she pursues apart from a few new blouses or shirts she buys annually and her daily ration of sweet cakes. Her house is her biggest and only pride of ownership.

Mary Kelly has never known a man in the Biblical sense. Her brother lives on the edge of town but she hasn't seen him for years. A man her own age, two doors down, comes over to stack her firewood in the shed out back. They talk about the weather, local politics and thanks be to God who has kept them going all these years. She does her best to avoid all the other neighbours.

Mary has straight grey hair framing a long grey face that droops like a well used tea towel over an oven door. It hasn't worn a smile for years, maybe decades. Like her shapeless slightly bent form, so is her life, a daily unchanging featureless routine leading inevitably to its surely unnoticed end.

Mary was sitting outside her kitchen window listening to the radio, waiting for her cousin and his wife to arrive. She fussed over her blouse and skirt and shifted in her chair, moving a little deeper into the shade on this rare glorious sunny Irish summer day. She was mumbling at the moment she lifted her eyes and found herself looking at two faces peeking around the corner. Jack and Sharon had been watching her in silence for about half a minute. She jumped from her chair, at once surprised and delighted to see them.

"What are you doing spying on me like that? Are you trying to frighten me to death?"

She smoothed her skirt as Jack approached and took her in his arms for a long embrace. "I've invited your neighbour to come over for a visit."

She pushed him back. "Och, you're such a troublemaker, so you are," she said mischievously while nodding her head towards the upstairs window. "Don't be talking too loud, she'll hear you."

She hugged Sharon then pulled the chairs closer to the wall.

"Sit down, sit down. I can't take the sun, sure I can't. Sit down. Where are you staying?"

"We're in Wexford on a home exchange," said Sharon. "We called here last Wednesday but you were out. Did you get our note?"

Mary didn't acknowledge the question.

"Would you like to see my shed? There's enough turf and wood to keep me going now for a whole year," she explained pride of preparation evident in her voice. Jack was expressing his admiration at how evenly the wood and turf were stacked when Mary suddenly turned the radio off, took his arm and walked towards the door. "Come in, come in."

The next hour was passed catching up on lives since their last visit a few years earlier 'though little had changed for Mary. "I always look forward to your

Christmas card and always reply, so I do. I used to write to your sister but she hasn't sent me a card for years so I don't write anymore. They don't contact me, I don't contact them," she said bitterly as she went to the tiny kitchen of her tiny house. "Now don't follow me. There's not enough room for two bodies in here. Are you hungry? You must be hungry. Would you like some tea? How do you like your tea, Sharon?"

"Not too strong please."

"Alright then, I'll boil it only a minute, so I will."

Jack and Sharon surveyed the space around them noticing the sacred pictures, phoney landscapes and the few pieces of delicate tea service inside a small glass cupboard. There was a stove insert in the fireplace with a water boiler in the lower part of the chimney. This was typical in these houses as a method of providing hot water. Mary dropped four teabags into the kettle of boiling water then reset the boil. "Go and wash your hands. There's no hot water. The weather's been shocking hot for the last two days so I haven't lit the fire."

"How much heat do you need?" asked Jack.

"I like to bring it to 600 degrees."

Sharon was startled. "Every day of the year?"

"If I want hot water," said Mary. "That's why me shed is full. "Do you put butter on your bread?" She brought a dinner place with eight slices of thickly buttered soda bread to the table. "Now." Two mugs were filled with the twice-boiled black as molasses liquid. Jack remembered Mary saying tea should be thick enough for a mouse to dance on. Mary said she didn't like to eat or drink with her guests.

She went back to the kitchen and returned with ham slices and cheese apologizing for having nothing to feed her visitors. "Go on. You must be starving after your long drive from Wexford."

Jack and Sharon did their best to please Mary who watched them eat and drink but not at the rate she would have wished. Another trip to the kitchen and another plate arriving piled high with Jaffa cakes and cupcakes.

"More tea, Jack? I was down to the post office when you came the other day. I used to walk all the time, out the Dublin road, you know, to the cemetery and back in along the Sarsfield Street. About six miles very day, so I did. But now I find it a pain just to go to the post office. Me knees are buggered with arthritis. All that walking all my life and where did it get me? I can't even go downtown. Eat up."

Sharon was struggling with the tea as Jack started into another slice of soda bread.

"Did you make the bread, Mary?"

Mary was massaging her knees, a faraway look in her eyes. Sharon touched Jack's arm and gestured towards their host who had gone deep into memory, her eyes glistening with pooling tears. Minutes of silence passed as slowly as a rainy Irish morning. "Eat up Jack. I do miss me walking, so I do. I miss me walking."

Sharon tried to take the conversation in another direction. "We met the family we are exchanging with at the airport. They have three kids and have done several swops in Europe. This is their first one overseas. Do you ever travel Mary?"

"Of course I have. Me friend Doreen and me like to go to Portugal every two years. In the Spring. It's warm but not too hot then."

She went to a desk and pulled out a package of photographs. One by one she held them up and gave a description. There was a sameness in all the photos; the white sun-drenched facade of a hotel or apartment with Mary or Doreen, a distant almost unrecognizable figure, their white blouses and skirts blending like whitewash into the walls. So far as could be seen, Mary didn't ever smile for the camera.

"I save me money for the trip. I've already got enough for next May."

"They're lovely pictures Mary," said Sharon. "So bright, so sunny. It looks like you're having a great time."

"How long has it been since your last visit, Jack?" Mary asked.

"The last time we were in Ireland was in 2010 so its been six years and that was on an exchange too."

"That long," said Mary. "It seems like only yesterday. Are you coming back next year? You'll come and visit me, so you will." It was more a command than a request.

"Of course we'll come, God willing," Sharon said with forced enthusiasm.

"We'd better get on the road," said Jack rising from his chair. He gave Mary a prolonged hug.

"You'll not forget to send me a card at Christmas, so you won't," she said.

"We always do Mary. Why would you think we'd forget you?"

She saw them to the door then went inside to wave goodbye from the window.

Elephants

Who doesn't celebrate the arrival of new life? Everything changes in an instant: decisions never encountered before become paramount, new schedules arise, strange sights and sounds and smells permeate the once neutral serenity of the home, the hours between daybreak and nightfall blur into a great unmeasurable lump of time, personal privacy becomes a memory, vacations are written off, going out means grocery shopping and television ads for anti-anxiety remedies become prime-time viewing. Yes, who doesn't love the arrival of new life?

Before this dramatic change intruded itself into Brian's life he had invited his parents over to help insulate the basement. He was still reasonably happy and rational despite being deeply in debt. Eight months earlier he took on a mortgage for the first time with an added forty thousand dollar estimate for badly needed upgrades and renovations. His credit line was stretched to the limit, a burden alien to Brian who had always managed his finances with competence. Strapping and insulating the basement was an inexpensive first step and would help reduce heating bills during the approaching second winter in his new home.

Brian and his Dad were almost finished unloading the materials when the next door neighbour arrived with a couple of beers. Pierre had spoken to Brian once or twice, nothing more than a friendly greeting, but this time he clearly meant to have a conversation. After a few polite meaningless words he introduced his agenda. He was concerned that his small meticulously cared for garden was sooner than later going to be overcome by Brian's gravel driveway which rests on ground two feet higher than his perennials. There needed to be a retaining wall, a very costly retaining wall built along the thirty feet of property line and he was offering to share the cost with Brian.

Pierre is ninety years old but his intellect and confidence remain sharp as a tack. Early on in his professional career he was a veterinarian who quickly established himself into the community's social and political life and was noticed. The prime minister's office invited him to participate in a "think tank" on environmental issues and he stayed there for nearly a decade after which he shaped a committee to safeguard the thousands of trees that defined the local living space. This committee succeeded to the point where the nearby university acquired his expertise and soon a new program on arbour studies had been shaped into existence. When it became a school of studies, Pierre's name was engraved on a plaque. With this sort of success behind him, he was accustomed to having his proposals embraced and this was evident in the way he directed the conversation that afternoon. Brian's Dad did his best to hold him off while his son continued unloading lumber under the weight of a headache that seemed to have come from nowhere.

But one man's priority shouldn't become another man's crisis and despite knowing Brian didn't own a car and was tied up in winterizing his home, Pierre pressed the urgency of the retaining wall.

When Brian's sister Brenda heard about the basement project she decided she would like to help. She also decided it would be a brilliant idea to bring a better-late-than-never housewarming gift, a gift carefully selected to bring a smile to her brother's face, stir memories of his favourite childhood books and provide him with months, maybe even years of companionship. She brought him a rabbit, an adult white furred, pink-eyed bunny with its own living quarters and enough food to last a week or so. Her car pulled into the driveway just as Pierre disappeared into his house and filled with joyful anticipation she carried the cage into the living room while Brian was downstairs. When he came up and saw his new houseguest he stopped and stared wide-eyed like a deer caught in headlights. Before he could say anything, Brenda had thrown her arms around him and was babbling about Peter Rabbit and Thumper and Fiver and now with his own real live rabbit he could hug him and kiss him and call him George. She took the rabbit out of its cage and pressed it into her brother's arms. Slowly he regained his composure and started stroking its back much to Brenda's satisfaction. He admitted he liked the gift, the bunny, but would have to learn how to care for it and wondered how much time that would require each day.

He was soon to find out.

Brenda bade Brian goodbye next morning, their parents staying on to wrap up the job. The second day, after supper, Brian brought the still-unnamed rabbit into the living room and was allowing it to explore and climb over him when he suddenly leaped from the sofa sending the animal flying across the room like a white shot put. The rabbit dove under a chair for cover. Brian looked at his shirt, at the wet patch which wasn't there a moment ago, then at the sofa decorated by dozens of small black pellets. Happily his mother wasn't in the room to hear what he had decided to name the bunny and happily the bunny didn't understand the meaning of language. After the cleanup the rabbit was unceremoniously returned to its cage and Brian went looking for some aspirin.

Brian's mother picked up the phone on the fifth ring about a week later and after saying hello was seen by her husband to listen quietly for nearly a full minute then collapse into hysterical laughter, waving the phone at arm's length for him to take. It was Brian still pouring a torrent of torment and expletives, torture and excitement— not the good kind— down the corridor of cyber communication. His father moved the phone away from his ear and waited for Brian to catch his breath before speaking to him. By now his wife had reclaimed self-control and it was his turn to lose it. The rabbit's cage had been left open yesterday while Brian was at work and it had committed two unforgivable crimes.

First, it had eaten holes in the covers of books stacked on floor level shelving. Secondly it had dropped eight babies into the shavings piled at one corner of its cage.

Brian had to raise his voice to ask his father what was so funny, who at last replied he should call the rabbit Pierre, move the cage to the basement and start charging her rent.

Brian was not amused.

Dogs

Mickey was my one and only dog. If you asked my brother or two sisters about Mickey they would make the same claim; Mickey, each would say, was my dog.

He wasn't a big dog nor was he an animal that would draw, "Oh, what a beautiful dog!" sighs from admirers. Think of a fire hydrant only horizontal with four feet and a stubby tail completely clothed in short black hair. No colour at all. Black as coal with coal black eyes.

When we got him he was about three years old, a hybrid made of 100% muscle, 100% loyalty, 100% Go with no Pause button, 50% stupid, 50% smart and 100%

protective of his food dish. If you even looked at him while he was eating he would curl his upper lip to reveal a sabre-tooth incisor and growl two deep but meaningful growls. Whenever he gave this warning, we gave him wide berth.

Mickey was the most wonderful dog! Wouldn't hurt a flea if he had one and he hadn't. Treated people and other dogs alike, as playmates. Started his day at full throttle and didn't stop until he collapsed into sleep. In short he was the archetypical wonderful dog that every dog owner owns.

There was a Christmas when more booze than food was consumed by the too many adults crowded into our small kitchen. Come to think of it, most Christmases that I remember at home were like that. I was the oldest child at 16 I think, and I was told to keep Mickey out of the way. At supper I sat at the corner of the table with Mickey behind me close to the wall. He could smell the lovely aromas of roast turkey wafting through the house and he began to drool so I put a dish of food under his nose. The man next to me was watching through an 80 proof alcoholic fog which I swear hovered around his head like a beekeeper's hood.

"Wha......wha.....a...gra....gra.....dog," he faltered as he reached to stroke Mickey's head.

There was neither a lip curl nor a growl, just the swift savage crush of canines on human flesh. The man looked in shock at the torn skin and blood which a second ago had been the palm of his hand. Surprisingly he didn't scream.

He just kept looking at his hand while everyone else refilled their glasses. I shoved a serviette into the bloody mess and led him to the door, grabbed a set of car keys and took him to the hospital. The on-call physician stitched and bandaged the wound and gave him a shot of antibiotics.

"This guy's so pickled he probably doesn't need this," he chuckled. The nurse didn't try to hide her amusement.

Some people are quick studies, some are slow learners and some never learn at all. Not five minutes inside the door, our patient decided to approach Mickey; same hand, same result, second trip to the hospital. This time the doctor was not making wise cracks.

"What the hell were you thinking?" he roared. "Maybe I shouldn't treat you! Maybe I should throw you out and wait for you to come back again so I can amputate!" But treat him he did and I drove him to his own house for his safety.

Next Spring we moved to a 'No Pets' townhouse. Nothing good would come of this. We were forced to give Mickey to the Humane Society and never saw him again.

Two years later I, along with three friends, went back to our favourite fishing lake for an early Autumn holiday. We preferred this time of year because all the tourists were gone and the lake was empty of boats. We were going to a burger joint for lunch and there was an Irish Setter snoozing outside the entrance. I was the last one in line. Nothing good could come of this. Unprovoked she suddenly jumped and bit me under the left shoulder blade.

"Why me?" I cried. "I'm Irish too!" I guess she didn't like Republicans.

The proprietor and owner of the dog looked at the tear in my sweater and threw a twenty-dollar bill at me.

"Get yourself a new sweater," was all he said as we left to find another place to eat.

Several decades have slipped away since these bittersweet dog tales and I have avoided any further close encounters, that is until two years ago. One of my daughters insisted on bringing her dogs with her to my house for Christmas. I should have been wary but she said they were family and would not be left behind so I acquiesced.

When they arrived the dogs were released into the house and immediately made themselves known. Think of two brown and black coffeemaker-size critters who, instead of pouring out soothing lattées, dispense high octane anxiety and do so with impunity. Nothing good could come of this either. Boxing Day morning I cleaned up their liquid and solid anxiety from the dining room floor while they looked on dispassionately.

At that moment I unleashed all the pent-up fury which had been compartmentalized and sealed in my memory banks for more than half a century since I lost Mickey and was bitten by the Irish bitch. Nostrils flaring, fists clenched and eyes narrowed to slits of disdain I spat out the words, "Bad dogs."

Needless to say they will never be welcomed back.

Dogs, dogs, dogs. The world has gone to the dogs! They eat better than many humans, have their own wardrobes, groomers, physicians, psychiatrists, stylists, whisperers, pamper products and even dedicated dog resorts. I was shopping at a local business last week and when I told the salesman I had walked over. He said, "But where is your dog?"

Christmas is fast approaching again and we expect four children, six grandchildren, to be here for a grand dinner in the style of Christmases gone by when we would be blessed with 20 or more family members around the table. It is going to be great!

Yesterday I made some telephone calls to firm up loose ends like times of arrival, accommodation needs and so forth. A daughter, sister to the two waste disposal units owner, reminded me she has a dog. Think of a piano bench with blond hair, long legs and bulk of body who stands in the kitchen. Stands and intimidates. Leans against your legs and waits.

This dog is part of her family too. No dog, no daughter, no grandchildren.

Nothing good can come of this.

As an aside, but not completely unrelated, I do believe in conspiracy theories.

Secrets

Maudie and God had a secret, a real secret because neither one of them told anyone else and I just figured it out a week after her funeral. I'm the only one in the world who knows it because none of the others noticed and as I was Gran's favourite, I figured it out when I was thinking about the secrets we shared the last years of her life. The others don't know about them either.

At the funeral the young priest, all polished and shiny in his crisp white linen alb and a glow of peach fuzz where he hoped a beard would grow, was uneasily trying to say something about a woman two generations his senior and whom he had met only a few times during his visits to the Seniors Care Home. He stood beside her coffin with a silver bucket of holy water and a silver sprinkling wand as big as a hammer. I don't know if he was paying homage to her or scolding the congregation and the world at large.

"She was proof.
She was living evidence of saints and saintliness.
A woman whose life went unnoticed,
but not by God.
She was born, lived and died next door to any of us.
To all of us.
All you know of her, all the world will remember of her is the short dash
between the year of her birth and the year of her death."

The young priest, our recently arrived new pastor was inexperienced at homilies and sermons but not with the use of holy water, a sacramental he obviously believed should not be spared. When he carefully dipped his thumb into the silver bucket and traced a cross on Gran's coffin, I thought that was her final blessing, a gentle gesture reflecting the sanctity of the moment. But then he wrapped his fist around the sprinkling wand and like the

God of Noah's ark, liberally splattered a great cascading overflight of holy water on and around Gran's ark, a eulogy of Biblical proportions for everyone to see and be wetted by. After the first shower, hands covered faces, heads cowered and gasps of shock and surprise rolled around the pews. The heavenly rain continued until droplets were dripping from the coffin onto the floor and the closest mourners had finished mopping their faces with tissues and handkerchiefs. The young priest brought the moment to an end with a rather satisfying chanted "Amen," then stepped back as two men moved in, one fore, one aft to navigate Gran down the centre aisle to the church entrance where waited the hearse and the last long mile.

My Gran grew up in Mennonite country. Her father was an anomaly, a non-Mennonite farmer who owned a car, a Ford, in the midst of horses and carriages and dark clothed old order Martins and Webers and Snyders. She loved her father's car. She would say to him, "Can we go somewhere in The Ford today, Daddy?" She liked to say "The Ford". It sounded strong and firm to her, not like other less certain cars like Dodges and Chevys. She loved it when, on Sundays they would drive past a long line of Mennonite horse-drawn buggies, sedans and broughams carrying men in black shiny suits and women wearing full length dark dresses and broad brimmed bonnets that reminded her of the coal scuttle back home. She noticed the boys and girls her age never seemed to smile when she waved to them from the safety of The Ford. She thought they were cheerless all the time and dressed like that in black wagons made it look like they were all going to a funeral. My Gran was suspicious and a little afraid of Mennonites but she didn't know why.

When she finished high school my Gran— Maudie— was wooed by a young architect from the city whom she met in the nearby town. She thought him to be more sophisticated than the ordinary fellows she knew, 'though she had no idea what he saw in her. "Maybe he saw something in me I didn't," she told me once, "And when he looked into my eyes and called me 'darlin,' I was a goner."

They were wed in less than a year and honeymooned for a four day weekend in a posh hotel in the city. When they moved into a two bedroom cottage with a hardened dirt floor, she didn't complain. Her new husband promised it was for the short term and when the money started rolling in he would buy her a proper house. Before long she was expecting their first child and her husband had opened a small office in town where he spent a lot of his time. Within five years they had three children. One day her husband brought his ailing father home as if it was the most natural thing and set him up in a cot in the living room space. Maudie had no say in the matter.

My Gran told me these stories as if they were distant events, as if she had not lived them herself. There would be long silences and she would stare past me trying to recover details, I thought, before talking again. She never seemed angry or sad, just resigned to her place in life as a mother of ten children rather than a wife or lover to her husband.

There were eight people living in the overcrowded cottage when the war came and being skilled and successful as an architect, her husband was recruited as a camp and buildings designer. He gathered some of his things together, saluted and walked out the door. This was the first of only two times I saw traces of anger in her eyes and her teeth clenched. She must have felt abandoned or even unloved when he left so abruptly without arranging for her security. But he did send home his first cheque and the number of a small bank account she could draw on, making her feel guilty for her feelings and a little more hopeful for his homecoming.

Just before the war ended, her father-in-law died and the funeral home sent a black hearse to remove his body. It was an encounter with death that startled her, she told me because it was so close and immediate. We were sitting in the common room of the seniors home when she took my hand and pulled me closer as if to tell a secret.

"I had a dream that night.

A bad dream.

I dreamed there was a long line of hearses, dozens of them, all black Mennonite carriages pulled by black horses and his body was in each one of them.

It was a terrible dream."

I have to admit I was a little frightened myself by that story and Gran must have noticed. "Don't worry," she said. "I don't mean to scare you. I tell you these things because you're my favourite." I guess it was because I was her youngest granddaughter and knew about secrets between youngest and oldest. I loved my Gran. I really do miss her.

There was a smell I can't describe in Gran's residence, the smell of old people's parchment skin, drool-soaked bibs, incontinence, and death. I never let it interfere with my visits or was less cheerful to her because I wanted to hear her stories. When her own children grew up and left I was her only regular visitor since I was about ten years old. I hated going into that place. Too many people there were old or sleeping in their chair or saying the same thing over and over.   Only my Gran seemed real and didn't deserve to be in that awful smelly dying place. I really loved her and wish she had had a better life, especially a kinder husband.

The second time I saw my Gran angry, it was I who cried and snuggled into her arms to find comfort and understanding for both of us. She said it was the worst year of her life.

"My curiosity got the better of me.

I found a note on his desk in his office.

It was from a woman.

They were to meet for lunch.

But I took the youngest kids and got there first and gave her a piece of my mind, I did."

A long silent pause from my Gran, me holding back the tears.

"That was July. In October my beautiful third son died a few days after his sixteenth birthday."

361

I had heard about this event, still I remained silent and clung to her frail frame.

"He came to the funeral and sat at the back of the church wearing sunglasses. He left early.

I never saw him again.

My boy was taken away in a black hearse.

I hate hearses.

When I die promise you won't let them take me away in a hearse."

All I could do was sob and hold on.

I'm telling you all this a week after her funeral but there's a smile on my face and here's why. It is the secret between God and my Gran which is my secret now and it is very funny. If she could have watched her own funeral with me, we would have laughed together.

When her coffin was slid into the hearse, the driver jumped into the front seat and turned the key but it wouldn't start. They looked under the hood and tried again but it was dead. Somebody ran into the church to tell the young priest and he came out and went straight to the driver.

"Take my car," he said. "It is a minivan. You can fold down the seats and the coffin will fit in." The driver agreed and the priest disappeared. A moment later he pulled his minivan around and parked it alongside the useless hearse. Under the lip of the bonnet attached to the grill in chrome letters was the word 'Ford.'

Stag

Whoever named the village Valemount lacked an historic or whimsical imagination. A few commercial buildings, some homes, paved streets, a doctor, dentist, a church and a couple of cops to keep the 1,000 souls safe make up the community. Valemount British Columbia hunkers at the base of three mountain ranges, the Cariboo to the west, Monashee to the south and the great Canadian

Rocky Mountains to the east, a settlement in a valley surrounded by sharp-edged ridges and snow-capped peaks; "Vale" - "Mount." A six-year-old could have come up with that and there must be hundreds of similar "Vale - Mounts" around the world. No imagination.

David Thompson stopped here in 1811 to set up a post for the North West Fur Trading Company and to build canoes from the abundance of birch trees in the area. He called the small river that flowed into the greater Columbia, Canoe River. Another slow-witted choice.

Consider this; Valemount lies at the north end of Kinbasket Lake, a 260km reservoir stretch that becomes Canoe Reach and stops short of flooding the village. Kinbasket was the name of the chief of the indigenous Shuswap people who trapped beaver for Mr. Thompson. It's his name that identifies the lake but Valemount could have been called Kinbasket, British Columbia or Shuswap, British Columbia in keeping with historical significance. And those names are much more evocative and decisive than is Valemount. Even a little tinkering with the surrounding mountains might have yielded "Sheebooky," or "Rosheeboo," or Carimoshee," British Columbia, great sounding names that anyone would be proud to call home. These monikers have shoulders and stories and bulk whereas Valemount belongs alongside Riverdale or Meadowlee and other bland street names in any Central Canada suburbia.

Valemount in the mountains is simply a breach of propriety, a misplaced micro-metropolis where no red-blooded Canadian young man would deliberately go rampaging through the remaining hours of freedom before bidding them "adieu" then succumbing to the shackles of "I do."

But Turlough came close, literally and figuratively the last week of June. Turlough - "dark lake" in the Irish, a real man name - climbed out of the car where the foot of Mount McKirdy dips into the lapping shore waves of Kinbasket Lake along with eight other real men here for a two day, two night stag party. The campsite was several kilometres out of sight of Valemount but equally distant from other camping areas and out of range of cell phone, internet, WIFI and other IT services. In short they were here on retreat from all things civil.

The group comprised two philosophers, two software engineers, two swing dancers, two writers and one salesman, a typical outdoor adventure camp ranging in age from 20s to 40s. But they were well prepared and equipped for the great huzza with three tents, boxes of beefsteaks and pork chops and an ambitious quantity of whiskey and vodka. Not surprisingly overlooked were more mundane items such as insect repellant and toilet paper.

Their first impression, as they later all agreed, was a lasting one. Their first impression was taken in the stillness of the early evening hours. It was the understated and omnipresent music of the mountains. Stood in this magnificent amphitheatre shaped by the hand of God in the Canadian Rockies, turned toward the three peaks, the river valley disappearing behind them, they heard the mountains sing and were themselves moved to silence. They heard water from melting snows meander and swish and splash and gurgle and whisper and wash over, around and through hundreds of channels etched into the mountainsides long before they arrived. They heard the wind shimmer and shudder the birch leaves then surge and sigh among languorous evergreen boughs before gathering itself into a sudden swift updraft against rocky outcrops and ledges. They heard this music and loved the moment forever.

One of them broke the reverie by challenging everyone to a skinny dip in the icy-cold water of the lake. Those who thought it was a great idea were grateful for those who did not and were busy setting up tents but more importantly, had organized a big blazing campfire. In short order all were tucking into man meat meals and praising the warmth of whiskey on a cool mountain evening.

The last spectacle to behold before succumbing to fatigue was the unpolluted coal-black northern night sky and the billions of crystallized stars and galaxies encircling the surrounding peaks. They moved slightly beyond the campfire to lie on their backs and gaze in true amazement into the unimaginable depths and wonders of space. Eventually someone mumbled goodnight and one-by-one they sought their sleeping bags and tents. The first day had come to a satisfying end.

No one was first to get up but everyone started day two the same way, cursing the mosquitos and other mountain insects that had feasted on their faces and limbs while they slept. But, of the two necessities they had forgotten to bring, bug repellant was the least inconvenient as they began to discover after breakfast and throughout the rest of the adventure. These men were really roughing it in the bush.

Mount McKirdy rises 2,586m or about 7,800ft above sea level and as it was in their neighbourhood it sounded like a good plan to scale it. After all, they were already standing well above sea level so the peak was therefore, much closer than the numbers suggested. The decision was unanimous and the ascent began after a fortifying lunch of beef and booze. Nature has a way of separating the fit from the feeble and in a few hours an inviting plateau was about to be won by the two leading climbers. Five others were still scrambling over boulders and screes a little below and bringing up the rear 15 minutes behind, the last pair struggled for foothold. When all had assembled on the landing and caught their breath and bearings the mountain top still seemed no closer even 'though they reckoned they had climbed some 1,500m, or about one and a half kilometres, a remarkable feat indeed and congratulations were plentiful and loud. There emerged an unspoken agreement that this was as far as they would go and the group began a reconnaissance for the safest way down, all but one and he was standing on the precipitous edge of the plateau looking down a sheer drop of hundreds of metres of cliff face. Carefully and deliberately he shed his garments and prepared to exercise an ablutionary discharge that only men can do standing up. Arms outstretched like an olympic diver on a high platform preparing to throw himself into the abyss, he released all restraints and as the amber liquid streamed and steamed into the cold Rocky Mountain air, he emitted that great primeval cry on behalf of all men, past, present and future, the cry of assurance, self-knowledge and the singular cocksure oneness with nature.

It was in the midst of this great twofold proclamation of unfettered affirmation that an equally great wallop of air blasted against the cliff in a sudden upward trajectory blessing the primal priest with his own holy water.

When they had overcome the initial shock of what they were witnessing, the onlookers all at once collapsed into uncontrolled laughter holding themselves and each other, pointing at the object of their exuberance, falling to their knees, laughing themselves senseless. It was all too funny, too funny for any one to think of reaching for a camera. It was a moment between man and nature; man had given of himself to nature and nature had given itself back to man.

At base camp the consensus was to clean up and go into Valmount for a meal. The village is bounded on the west by the Southern Yellowhead Highway and on the east by Whiskey Fill Road. As they walked the latter corridor they chuckled at the irony of the name. The Three Ranges Brewing Company looked inviting as did their local beers with names such as Swamp Donkey Brown Ale and the historically colourful Tail Slap IPA with a label depicting a robust beaver holding its broad flat tail. At least the proprietor of this small business seems to have gotten it right.

One more night under the stars capped off by vodka shooters and donations to the mosquito blood supply ended an uneventful stag party never to be forgotten. There's an understanding that hikers or campers going into the wilderness should never leave anything behind them and take out nothing but pictures. There is no photographic evidence of the events that took place those two days in the mountains but if you ask Turlough who got married three days later, he'll tell you they were the best.

Maple Villa

This is a story, a very short sketch, actually, about a big house in a small village in Southwestern Ontario, Canada. Dear reader, before you get your knickers in a knot and say to yourself, "Who wants to read about bricks and mortar, wood and glass?" let me assure you it's worth the few moments required to read on to the end. At that point you may pass judgement in any direction you wish. So carry on for your greater edification and entertainment, then you are free to go.

First the boring bits.

The house was called Maple Villa by its builder who, in 1895 constructed his two-storey red brick Edwardian 2,400sq.ft. home on a property 120ft. x 140ft. surrounded by 13 maple trees. He had some money for when it was completed Maple Villa was a centre piece of the village for several decades with its carved maplewood front door, maplewood floors, bay windows, five with stained glass and two staircases, the grander one at the front for family use and the narrower concealed stairway that led from the kitchen to the maid's small room situated in a corner far away from the upstairs commerce of the family.

Seen from above, the five bedroom house has a cruciform north-south alignment, the front door facing south, the Patibulum running east-west at the rear of the house where the morning room and kitchen are located. The maid's stairway is accessed via a nondescript door in one of the kitchen's corners allowing her to unobtrusively arrive downstairs and have breakfast prepared long before the family came down. All this and other similar class defined practices took place in a bygone era when, for better or worse, the inhabitants of Maple Villa owned a sense of proportion.

Bye-the-bye, almost one hundred years later when alongside a neighbour I was digging a compost hole at the boundary of our two yards, we came upon an earthenware urn some three feet into the ground. Referring to municipal records we discovered we had disturbed the mortal remains of the house's original owner. As there was no maid hovering nearby, we put him back ourselves where his remains remain to this day.

When we purchased Maple Villa in 1983, we understood we were the fifth owners in fact but in reality only the fourth occupants as the sellers never lived there. Along with our four children we were also following a trend of large families living in the house throughout its history. By the time we left our long term now empty nest home in 2014, we had raised seven children and were considered by the modern villagers as eccentric. (Neither resentment nor bitterness implied.)

We sold our home to a three-generation family, maternal grandparents, mom and dad and four grand/children. A few months into their ownership they described Maple Villa as "Our forever home," echoing our own sentiments more than 30 years earlier and continuing the form of occupancy by kooky families.

And now dear reader, as promised, here are some of the more interesting pieces that set the house apart, at least during our sojourn.

Maple Villa is a double brick structure, all external walls having two layers of brick separated by a six-inch airspace supposed to act as insulation but doesn't. Our first winter there was a cold one indeed. Came the Spring we tore down all the plaster from these walls, installed fibre insulation, rebuilt the kitchen -dry goods were stored in a wheelbarrow in the dining room- while our fifth child was enduring her first weeks out of the safety of the womb. Within five years we had completed our renovations and had settled into an orderly lifestyle even finding time for an occasional night out away from the children. But this soon brought about another challenge; babysitters rarely returned for a second hiring. The maid's stairs became a conduit for ghostly presences and spooky happenings. While the unsuspecting victim watched television in the front room, all her charges asleep upstairs, a kitchen light mysteriously came on or water started running from a tap or hollow voices called unknown names. Our children could never be accused of lacking imagination.

The house was a magnet for "strays" befriended by our older children who brought them home, usually at suppertime. They were always required to call their own parents to allay their worries. In Summer it was not unusual to find on the upper porch any number of sleeping bags stuffed with snoring teenagers who seemed to have materialized from the air overnight. After breakfast they and their bedding quickly evaporated silently and invisibly. One particular weekend while I was away, my wife was awakened by mischievous giggles as half-a-dozen pyjamad girls bounced on her bed tickling her feet and nose. She told me she might have recognized one or two of them from earlier visits.

In times of conflict and troubles a "Safe House" was a place where one can hide or rest while contemplating their next move. So it was when two of my former students, naive and lost little girls, sought refuge at Maple Villa. They needed a place to recover from their abortions before the inevitable return home and the confrontation they must have with their parents who had no idea where they had been for days. We comforted and counselled them as best as we could then drove them the long silent hour north to those who loved them most and awaited an explanation.

Super Sunday Suppers, multi-layered courses of exotic meals and fine wines were weekly teaching seminars where the family learned to appreciate and help organize the most favoured event of the week; food, wine, conversation, always entertaining, sometimes fiery and contested. Some of the "strays" heard about this tantalizing event and began to arrive on a regular basis eager to test new flavours and add to the wonderful mayhem. Our now adult children maintain these are the best memories they have of their time in our welcoming home.

In like manner our monthly family prayer cenacle became known to other families and in a few years Maple Villa regularly hosted as many as seventy men, women and children for an hour of prayer and pot luck eats. During the week between Christmas and New Year's, this event was favoured by the presence of our Bishop who braved the challenging Canadian winter roads for eleven consecutive years to pray and break bread with us. Those were cherished and spiritually uplifting starts to the New Year.

Maple Villa had a two-car garage, not configured as you might imagine with space for two cars side-by-side but for two cars end-to-end. We closed off the back half and turned it into a 20ft. x 20ft. family room. Here we held a wedding reception for one of our daughters who a few months later miraculously gave birth to a baby boy. Quelle surprise! Add twenty years and our youngest daughter under the tardy attendance of her midwife snoozing in the room next to her, brought her second son into the world at around four a.m. while I was trying to get some sleep. In the morning my wife, daughter and midwife formed a gang of accusers wagging index fingers and sharp tongues in my face and screeching something about neglected duties. To this day I don't have any idea what they were on about.

Another daughter married a musician of the roots-folk idiom. He is a Scot, or more accurately a descendant of my Irish forefathers who long ago colonized that cold rocky North Atlantic outcrop of lochs and bens, lairds and leals and a contemporary generation of young men and women eager to become the reincarnation of Robert Burns accompanied by never in the same key violin, guitar, accordion and bodhran. Aside: for the uninitiated, the latter is a wooden hoop covered on one side by skin from a dead goat which is struck by a "musician" holding a length of stick. It is pronounced 'bow rawn.' End of Aside.

Suddenly Scotland was effluencing a plethora of boy bands, girl bands, boy-girl bands and all of them knew our new son-in-law and how to get to Maple Villa. One day, I think it was shortly after the newlyweds returned from their honeymoon I happened to glance at the calendar on our kitchen wall. Seems we were hosting a house concert for a band called Calghleghia or some unpronounceable word like that which was touring Canada. I lifted the page to the next month where another band was pencilled in. Two more further on, all from Scotland. Calling upon my sense of duty to our Celtic cousins I spread the word and discovered hundreds of fans of Clagheligah and the rest who were eager to pay for the chance to hear them play in a very intimate and private venue. Who knew? The concerts were always evening events and they had to sleep somewhere so next day we fed them hot scones and boiled tea and sent them on their way.

Maple Villa was a happening place for decades and we were were merely its caretakers.

One of the steps taken when a property is transferred from one owner to another is an inspection of the premises by a home inspector on behalf of the buyer. In 2014 this report encouraged the prospective buyer to walk away from the deal. The stone and cement foundation was unreliable at best and could crumble into dust at any minute, the inspector warned. That was news to us, but the buyer was not convinced and hired a heritage building engineer to take a second and closer look. My wife and I, the buyer and his wife were drinking tea when he finished his two hour evaluation. What we expected was math and science but what he said was startling. He sat down, slapped the report on the table, poured a mug of tea and smiled at the four of us. "The walls of this house are embedded with love."

All things considered it was the very best thing anyone could ever say about Maple Villa.

Doolin

The music and the craic were gone for another year. Compared to the summer weeks when thousands of musicians and buskers and tourists and boozers turned this small West Ireland fishing village into the cosmopolitan cultural centre of Europe, the streets were deserted now, silent and dismal. Dismal due to the low ceiling of a cloudy North Atlantic grey-on-grey cold wet uninspiring weather front that had rolled across the region four days earlier and once settled, refused to budge.

Six September tourists had arrived with the meteorological misery expecting an Autumnal retreat, days of hiking and exploration of flora and fauna but that was never to be and they were leaving at the end of the week. Worse than that, there were two plump chickens roasting in the oven and only one bottle of wine on the table. Something had to be done before the off-license closed.

The rental cottage was a real find; a four bedroom recently built bungalow with all the mod cons, comfortable easy chairs, central heating, books, CDs a well equipped kitchen, and best of all, situated about five kilometres east of Doolin at the end of a narrow unpaved stretch of road with enough switchbacks to test a driver's skill and patience. The closest neighbour was well out of sight and sound guaranteeing solitude when needed and turn-the-volume-up-to-ten when wanted.

The four adults knew how to while away the hours when cabin bound, but two teenage boys were antsy and bored.

"Get in the car, lads, quickly and quietly," was all they needed to hear as their fathers grabbed their coats and headed out into the rain. The startup of the motor brought one of the women to the door.

"Where are you going?"

The driver rolled down the window, "To pick up women! Be back in a bit."

The boys jostled each other and laughed. "That's a good one Dad. Let's get outa here."

In Doolin they could have parked wherever they wanted but stopped near the docks where the boys could do a little exploring. Half an hour later six bottles of wine, some candles and napkins were secured in the boot and a blast on the horn brought the boys running.

"Can we go somewhere else? The cottage is boring."

"There's not much to do in this weather and the light is fading. We better get back. Maybe tomorrow."

There's a straight stretch of road before it starts its winding climb and with the fuchsia hedgerows pressing over the narrow shoulders, they drove slowly in the unlikely expectation that they might meet another vehicle.

"What's that up there, Dad? Looks like a cow or a horse."

They slowed to a crawl and steered to the right as the shape evolved into two backpacking hooded trekkers looking lonely and rain soaked as the world around them. When they heard the car they stepped into the middle of the road and waved frantically. A window was opened.

"Are you two lost?"

The boys leaned forward for a closer look.

"Do you know if there's a barn around here where we can stay the night?"

"Better than that," said the driver. "This is your lucky day."

His front seat side kick picked up the cue, hopped out and opened the boot.

"Put your gear in here, then climb aboard."

On another day when the sun was shining and hearts were light, the trekkers might not have waved, the driver not stopped, the encounter never arrived and everything that followed never taken place. But this was not another day and this is what happened.

All suspicion, hesitation, doubt, alarm, caution and timidity were cast aside as the two soggy intruders somehow managed to insert themselves between or upon the back seat boys, four bodies in a three seat space, limbs folded or tucked or splayed or wrapped around, and the greatest surprise of all from a startled teenage boy, "Holy moley Dad. They're girls!"

"Thank you for stopping," said the blonde shoving her hood back. "We could have been anybody, umm, dangerous," she added, her German accent cutting through the claustrophobic cramped quarters.

The other one, a brunette, added, "Yes. Thanks a lot."

The boys, glued uncomfortable close to their visitors tried to look at each other sideways. Their eyes and surreptitious smiles were communicating the same message about babes and opportunities and exotic accents and bodies, male and female tightly pressed against each other and prospects in the cottage and everything.

Up front the driver elbowed his co-pilot and nodded towards the back seat. Here they were a pair of married men with children wishing they were half their ages and unattached who just happened to pick up two women and were now driving to their isolated cottage. Four men drooling over two women on the rainy wild west coast of Ireland driving back to their mothers and wives.

At the cottage as the girls retrieved their packs and the men their purchases, the boys rushed straight inside. "Dad was right, Mom. We picked up women. And they're hot and have accents. This is going to be great!"

When the men and their new guests strolled into the cottage, their wives were speechless.

"They need somewhere to stay tonight and as we've got an empty bedroom....O.K?"

"I guess." And then the instinct of motherhood and protection took over. "Of course. You dears must be frozen. Put your stuff in there. Do you have any dry clothes? We'll make you a hot cup of tea."

"Could we have a bath first?"

"Yes. Yes. You probably haven't had a decent wash in days. Give us your laundry and we'll get it washed and dried. Go on, there's the bathroom."

About an hour later the table was set for a dinner party of eight with candles, wine and enough inviting food to drive the dank weather away outside and celebrate the serendipitous occasion inside. Everyone had changed their clothing, the boys in their best tops fidgeting nervously in the kitchen when the two girls entered in their flannel pyjamas. They had brushed their hair to cascade over their shoulders framing delightful smiles which lit up their rosy scrubbed faces. The men pretended not to notice, the women took them in an embrace and said, "You look wonderful." The boys stared as if their two favourite movie stars had stepped out of the screen and into their personal lives.

"Why don't we all sit down. You boys can have one of our guests each side of you and we will sit here. That O.K. with you dear?" And the men obeyed.

One of the boys seemed lost in a sort of reverie. "What's that nice smell?"

"It's the chicken," said Dad.

"No. I mean it smells….it smells like flowers."

The brunette giggled. "When we go trekking we always like to have good shampoo and soap. It makes us feel better when we can find a shower."

The boy blushed and took a drink of water. His Dad held up a bottle of Burgundy. "You girls are old enough to drink wine?"

"Yes we are. Thank you."

In a while the wine glasses were being refilled for the third or fourth time, - even the boys were permitted a sample. The food was praised and the conversation very relaxed.

"We have been sleeping wherever we could find shelter the past few nights and before you came along we were afraid we might not find anything tonight. This morning we were praying how wonderful to have a warm bed, a hot shower and some meat to eat instead of dried fruit. You are an answer to our prayers. We never believed this could happen. Not in a million years," said the blonde. They told stories of their travelling adventures in Ireland and where they lived in Germany and of expectations when they return to university next week.

That last detail fell on the boys like the final blow of defeat. They knew the girls were older than them but this confirmation finally burst the bubble of their dreams. The men remembered their own university days, and the reality of their ages which now expressed itself as deep sighs of what might have been under different circumstances.

The boys went to their room.

The men found comfy chairs and a bottle of whisky.

The four women pulled their chairs together, finished the wine, and when they finally ran out of laughter and things to talk about, piled the dishes in the sink before heading off to the security and warmth of a comfortable bed in the small hours of a cold and dreary Doolin night.

www.ingramcontent.com/pod-product-compliance
Lightning Source LLC
Chambersburg PA
CBHW060238100426
42742CB00011B/1573